Only
Mothers
Know

Recent Titles in
Contributions in Women's Studies

Only Mothers Know

Patterns of
Infant Feeding in
Traditional Cultures

DANA RAPHAEL *and* FLORA DAVIS

Prepared under the auspices of The Human Lactation Center, Ltd.

Contributions in Women's Studies, Number 54

Greenwood Press
Westport, Connecticut · London, England

To Margaret Mead whose lifetime was spent urging all of us ". . . about the importance of feeling responsibility to people we don't know yet and may never see."

Library of Congress Cataloging in Publication Data

Raphael, Dana, 1932–
  Only mothers know.

  (Contributions in women's studies, ISSN 0147-104X ;
no. 54)
  "Prepared under the auspices of the Human Lactation
Center, Ltd."
  Bibliography: p.
  Includes index.
  1. Breast feeding—Cross-cultural studies. I. Davis,
Flora. II. Title. III. Series.
RJ216.R32 1985   363.8'2   84-15742
ISBN 0-313-24541-X (lib. bdg.)

Library of Congress Catalog Card Number: 84-15742
ISBN: 0-313-24541-X
ISSN: 0147-104X

First published in 1985

Greenwood Press
A division of Congressional Information Service, Inc.
88 Post Road West
Westport, Connecticut 06881

Printed in the United States of America

10 9 8 7 6 5 4 3 2 1

CONTENTS

ILLUSTRATIONS

FOREWORD

When the renaissance of breastfeeding was just beginning, Dana Raphael wrote a sensitive, provocative book, *The Tender Gift: Breastfeeding,* that turned our attention to the needs of the new mother during the important rite of passage she calls matrescence. Through anthropological research and prodigious literature review she studied what makes for lactation success in other cultures and identified a major factor as the presence of a supportive person, a *doula.* The need for the doula, she pointed out, also exists in modern western cultures to enhance mothering skills by instilling confidence and providing nurturing.

Now, as interest and enthusiasm for breastfeeding broadens and mandates are created by professionals as well as official groups to increase the scope and duration of breastfeeding in western culture, Dana Raphael draws attention to the broader concepts of infant feeding thus tempering the passions of politicians and zealots. *Only Mothers Know: Patterns of Infant Feeding in Traditional Cultures* is contemporary anthropology at its best, embracing scientific method while using participant observations by field anthropologists to gather data in diverse settings. It is an accounting of real women with real babies coping with the real challenges of survival in third world countries and in a sample of underprivileged women in western cultures.

Through vignettes from ethnographers' field notes, insights into true feeding practices in seven countries are described as shared by the hundreds of women who revealed the actual events of raising their children and how they make their decisions about feeding. Raphael points out that "women will ultimately act in their own best interests and decide how to feed their babies according to what their lives will allow." Furthermore, the natural course of events when a mother responds to her baby's needs unencumbered by scientific data is to gradually add other foods. "Breastfeeding, though it conjures up a single activity as practiced by most mothers, is essentially a composite of behaviors," Raphael concludes.

Physicians, scientists, lactation experts and political leaders could gain considerable insight into the real issues of infant nutrition, breastfeeding and world hunger by reading this provocative account. Breastfeeding cannot be legislated but mothers everywhere need help in achieving what they wish for most—the best for their children. Raphael pleads with us to listen to these mothers who know the best way to keep their babies alive and then develop more flexible and humane food policies that will reduce the hunger and the malnutrition which is directly related to poverty in these cultures.

This is a very special report that should be read by the decision makers and fieldworkers interested in infant feeding in the modern world.

Ruth A. Lawrence, M.D.
The University Of Rochester Medical Center

ACKNOWLEDGMENTS

—to the hundreds of women who shared their lives and changed our minds, who made us angry but also filled us with admiration and affection for them;

—to the anthropologists in this study who cherished these women and worked selflessly so hard and long to make us understand the subtle and difficult patterns women must use to keep themselves and their children alive;

—to many like Joyce King, Hazel Tinsley, Elisabeth Cole, Frances Stout, Judith-Marie Buechler who became engrossed in the idea of revealing life as it is lived and contributed substantially to this book;

—to Flora Davis for her exhaustive study of the data and her excellence in digesting the material and making the lives of the women portrayed in the book so real;

—to Howard Boone Jacobson who helped us form the structure of the book and worked so tirelessly on style, syntax and tone;

—to Bristol-Myers Foundation whose funds contributed to the production of this book;

—to my family for their support when this research took me into other worlds and for their good humor when, exhausted and cranky, I returned to the fold.

I thank you all.

PREFACE

In the summer of 1976 a team of anthropologists carried out a unique study of breastfeeding. Working in eleven cultures scattered around the globe, from urban ghettos in the United States to villages in India, Egypt, and the Philippines, these fieldworkers lived in the communities, talked to mothers, observed hour after hour how they fed their babies—and came back with information totally at odds with popular assumptions.

At the time, researchers and health officials worldwide had suddenly become concerned because breastfeeding seemed to be declining in the developing countries and infant mortality to be on the increase. They put the two together—no breastfeeding leads to infant death. Many, including myself, were convinced that breastfeeding was being undermined by bottle feeding with commercial formula and that when mothers fed their babies this way they lost their breastmilk. Now the equation ran: Modern feeding methods, loss of breastmilk, dying babies.

Little did we know at the time that our intensive fieldwork would reveal that most mothers were still breastfeeding, that few babies of the poor were getting much additional food—no less processed milk. Equally surprising was our discovery that most Western trained professionals were largely unaware of how women in the lesser-developed countries (and poor women worldwide) actually fed their babies. Besides all that, few of us really appreciated these women's remarkable capacity to keep most of their children alive.

In the mid–1970s the Agency for International Development (AID), the foreign-aid wing of the U.S. government, received a mandate from Congress to find out what was happening to breastfeeding in the developing world. After months of talk, the then recently organized Human Lactation Center (HLC; I am the Director of the Center) received a grant to address that question. The grant was given to the center to compile and review all the relevant literature on lactation; to hold a conference that would bring together the top experts on infant feeding; and to analyze and publish our findings in a "summing up" of the state of the art of breastfeeding.

As an anthropologist I felt we could not know what was happening to breastfeeding unless we studied how it was practiced by real women with real babies in the course of their everyday lives. Most research until that time had focused on those women who were interviewed in clinics—mothers in crisis situations. So I persuaded the AID officers to let us spend a small portion of the grant to send anthropologists into the field to report firsthand observations of what was going on day to day in the home. Their reports produced the richest material and the greatest surprises. This book is a result of that original work.

To find researchers to take part in the study, we advertised in two anthropological journals. The ads specified "women only" since it is nearly impossible for male anthropologists to approach mothers in most cultures, much less talk to them about an intimate subject like breastfeeding.

The funds allocated were hardly enough to fund one anthropological field visit. However, thanks to Margaret Mead we used a model that helped us make the most of our limited resources. When she was about to go into the field, Dr. Mead would often write to colleagues and ask what they'd like her to find out for them. Thus, anthropologists who were interested in a cross-cultural study of dreams, or of cross-cousin marriages, could ask her to report on dreaming or marriages in New Guinea. She established a model for anthropological sharing and I used it—in reverse. I sought out fieldworkers who were already planning to spend the summer of 1976 in the field, and, in effect, I asked them to "piggyback" our research on their own studies in return for a small amount of money.

The women who joined the HLC study were professional anthropologists. Most of them taught at universities during the academic year and did fieldwork in the summers. They subsidized the field research with small grants and their own moneys. The studies they would pursue that summer, ranged from oral poetry and folklore to community organization, religious beliefs, and genetic factors in disease.

None of them had previously done research on breastfeeding practices, but that didn't matter to us. What was important from our point of view was that each would be *returning* to a community where she had worked before and where she had already developed bonds of friendship with other women. Thus she could come right to the point, ask them the most intimate questions and expect honest answers. She had laid the groundwork of trust over many years. Since they were her friends, the mothers were assured of anonymity and, once they understood the purpose of the study, generously shared their experiences. In the end these woman-to-woman relationships made possible the surprising insights the study revealed.

The first chapter of this book provides an overview of the fieldwork. It also describes some of my experiences as I visited the anthropologists in their community, for it was my task to supervise the fieldwork. It includes my own observations on breastfeeding, particularly in Jamaica, my first stop, and, like most "firsts," it holds my strongest impressions. This first chapter is a more personal account, in contrast to the rest of the book.

The next five chapters are taken directly from the ethnographers' field notes. The quotes from informants appear as they were written in the original reports. Each chapter is concerned with patterns of infant feeding in particular communities, and each features the life stories of several women. Through these vignettes readers are introduced to the cultures, learning not only how mothers go about feeding their babies but also why they do what they do and how their choices

fit the world they live in. Interspersed within these life stories
are the unexpected findings the studies revealed which will help
readers grasp the meaning of these often very complex behaviors. For to understand the status of breastfeeding today we
must see it in a broader context—and that means looking at
the way it meshes, or does not, with the needs and life goals
of the mother and her family.

Chapter 2 focuses on Igorot women, an isolated tribe in the
Philippines; Chapter 3 on village women in India and Egypt;
Chapter 4 on mothers in a mountain community in Sardinia;
Chapter 5 on young women from a tiny village in St. Kitts;
and Chapter 6 on black women in an urban housing project in
the United States. Though we did fieldwork in eleven cultures, we chose to concentrate on those six where the data lent
themselves most easily to the scenario format. They represent
the full range of cultural patterns in our study—from communities where breastfeeding was still universal to those where
most women bottle-fed. However, we want to recognize the work
of the other ethnographers who participated in this study and
from whom we drew findings which provided context for the
ideas advanced in this book. They are: Carol Bryant (Cuban
and Puerto Rican women in Florida); Catherine DiDominico
(market women, Nigeria); Renate Fernandez (shepherd villagers in Spain); Carmen Johnson (Chicano residents in
Houston); and Judith Johnstone (Moslem villagers from India
in Trinidad).

I want to emphasize that the information about infant feeding practices in these several cultures was drawn directly from
the anthropologists' field notes and as much as possible recon-
firmed by meetings or telephone calls during the writing of this
book. They are not composites. Each chapter was presented to
the fieldworker for correction and comments which were
gratefully incorporated into the manuscript.

Chapter 7 sums up my interpretations of what occurred when
breastfeeding became a political issue. It reviews what we
learned in the course of the study and what that knowledge
means for breastfeeding women.

The final text is a collaborative effort between myself and
Flora Davis, a professional writer. We use the first person sin-
gular "I" throughout because all the inferences, opinions and
conclusions drawn from the material are mine. They are based
on insights gained from my visits to the field sites and the responses of the hundreds of people I interviewed in seven different countries, including nurses, nutritionists, physicians,
ministers of agriculture and health, university professors, colleagues at several of the United Nations' affiliated organiza-
tions, representatives from industry and their critics in seven
different countries as well as a great variety of cooperative men,
women and even children.

Flora Davis must be credited with integrating the thousands of pages of field notes from this study with great skill
but her substantial talents with the book's narrative are what
makes each woman's personal story so engrossing.

Readers will find a great deal of human drama in this book
for it is not just about what is happening to breastfeeding. It's
about particular women, about hardship and courage and fun
and the wisdom of mothers who know—as their own mothers
knew—what keeps babies alive.

Only
Mothers
Know

1

BEYOND STATISTICS: THE ANTHROPOLOGICAL WAY

The breastfeeding project took two jam-packed years of my life. It was a hectic, exhilarating, often heartbreaking time that changed some of my most basic assumptions about poor women and breastfeeding mothers. At first, I bitterly resisted those changes. I'd reviewed shelves of scientific literature on lactation, conducted several original studies, even breastfed three children, and I felt I had a certain mastery of the subject. It was a humbling experience to learn just how much breastfeeding mothers in traditional societies could teach me.

Because these ideas are at the same time complex and subtle, I've gone into a great deal of detail in this chapter to explain how the research was done and how most of us on the team gradually developed a deepening sense of wonder at the creativity of women in poverty.

This breastfeeding study was unusual as anthropological research goes. Fieldworkers had certainly asked questions about breastfeeding in the past, but none of them had gone into the field to explore this subject in such depth as we did, nor had any study involved so many different communities all within the same few months. We were able to see patterns and make a kind of comparison never before possible.

The study was unusual in other ways, too. Fed by the energy and fascination of all those involved, it seemed to take on a life of its own, and it grew until it surpassed the scope of the original, relatively modest proposal. It was primarily due to the fieldwork aspect that it mushroomed. We sensed the excitement shortly after our notices were published announcing that we needed researchers. We received applications from many skilled anthropologists. So we kept increasing the number we hired while uneasily slicing the funding pie smaller and smaller. What a credit to our discipline that this challenge to work on a then new subject could raise such interest in these committed women.

Those of us who write grant proposals usually feel we have to plan out every detail of a study far in advance. Yet, in this case, the final approval, mired deep in government bureaucratic slowdown, had taken us into the spring. There we were, with time running out, the month of June and the summer fieldwork we counted on almost upon us. Faced with a deluge of talent, we just kept ad-libbing. From those hectic months that we spent organizing the fieldwork, one particular day stands out in my memory, perhaps because it illustrates so well our dilemma as well as our success.

It was a Saturday in May 1976. In the middle of the morning, I received a phone call from Sewanee, Tennessee, from a woman named Lee Stapleton who was responding to our notice. Lee explained that she and her husband, who was a minister and missionary, had lived for ten years in a remote, mountainous region of the Philippines among the Igorot, an isolated tribe, head-hunters just two generations ago. Two of her children had been born in the village; she had learned to speak the language and to love the people, and, in fact, she felt she had learned most of what she knew about mothering from the Igorot women. She wanted very much to be part of the study. If we could help fund her, she would pay for the rest and go back that summer.

I told her regretfully that we had already signed up all the anthropologists we could afford to take on, but I took her phone number and hung up. In point of fact, the original plan had been to send out five anthropologists. By the time Stapleton called me, we had committed nine. The funds available for fieldwork were already stretched beyond the limit.

Various Saturday chores were poorly done that day. All I

could think about was this woman who had lived with one of the few so-called primitive tribes left in the world. And she spoke the language! Before long, the anthropologist in me felled the budget director and I called Tennessee. If Mrs. Stapleton could manage on a small stipend, I wanted her to be part of the breastfeeding study.

And so it went. For me, it was an anthropologist's dream: a chance to study an important issue, explore cultural change, invent new research methods, and collect information sorely needed by ethnographers and health workers.

For the government officials at AID who funded us, the study promised to answer important political questions. They held the assumption, as did we, that babies were dying because breastfeeding was being undermined throughout the developing world due to a universal Westernization which inevitably included the introduction of baby formula. All of us fully expected that the study would gather evidence of this. Infant mortality was such a desperate and overwhelming problem, and health workers worldwide were so frustrated at their helplessness to do anything about it that they were only too eager to accept the idea that this devastating condition had a simple cause and a simple solution.

Breastfeeding had been a personal and professional preoccupation of mine for over twenty years. It started with my firstborn. Because I had seen women give birth in India and other countries, I was determined that everything about the birth of my child was going to be "natural." I insisted on natural childbirth, not yet popular, and of course I was also going to breastfeed, even less acceptable. As a typical American of that time, I had hardly thought about it, had never read anything on the subject, and knew no one in the United States who was breastfeeding. Still, I expected as a matter of fact that what mothers in other countries did—what mothers have always done—I would do, too.

Everything went according to plan except the breastfeeding. It didn't work. This child was hungry all the time, and the more he cried, the more anxious I felt; the more I nursed, the less milk I seemed to have. (How many women in New Delhi, Lagos, even Manila have I heard use those very words.)

I struggled with that baby, but in the end I had to give up. Depressed, furious and amazed, I turned to bottles. Most mothers in the world who fail at breastfeeding are not that lucky. Unless someone in the family owns a buffalo or goat who is giving milk, the baby is most likely to die. My compelling need was to know *why*. What went wrong? How had I failed? I went from library to library, reading everything I could find under breastfeeding and lactation. To my amazement, most of the literature was about cows! Now and then I pulled out some data on the physiology of breastfeeding and here and there a bit on the psychology of postpartum women.

At the time I was studying anthropology at Columbia University, so it was natural that I looked at the literature in that field as well. I went to the Human Relations Area File, HRAF as we call it, where hundreds of ethnographies have been broken up and classified under a thousand different headings. By looking up everything listed under #844 (childbirth), #853 (breastfeeding) and #862 (weaning), I learned what ethnographers had to report about the perinatal period in 276 human societies.

Oh my, what stories I read! Mothers who breastfed until the child was eight! Women who put feces on their breasts to make the child desist, and Islamic fathers who beat their wives if they could not (would not) breastfeed. Largely folklore, most of the information about breastfeeding began and ended with a curt comment on how many months women nursed and whether or not they thought colostrum was good for the baby. (Colostrum is the fluid the breasts produce for a few days after birth, before the "true" milk comes in.) However, one thing struck me: In all cultures where most women routinely breastfed their babies, the anthropologists had carefully recorded the series of gifts the mother received from family and friends and the elaborate rituals that were performed during the first few weeks or even months after the baby was born. I puzzled over these fairly universal patterns. Was it possible that one function of this attention was to ensure that the new mother had a kind of hiatus from her usual daily activities while lactation was being established?

As I was working on human patterns, Margaret Mead, my

chief advisor, prodded me into becoming the first anthropologist to use the ethological material (that is, descriptions of animals in their natural habitat) to help explain behavioral patterns in human beings. I found that among other mammals, elephants, chimps and dolphins for example, when a female is in labor and just after she has given birth, other females hover around and frequently interact in such a way as to help the mother care for her newborn.

Slowly it dawned on me that there was something about having others near and helpful that might be essential to successful lactation. I began to work on the idea that if breastfeeding is to succeed there must be someone around to mother the mother. One day I was describing this pattern to a friend of mine who politely translated our conversation to her eighty-five-year-old Greek mother-in-law. The woman interrupted us to explain how in her day in Greece a *doula*, usually a female relative or a neighbor, came to the home of the new mother, washed up the dishes, gave the other children a bath, and encouraged the mother, telling her how plump the baby was. Since there is no word in English to describe a person who performs this service, from then on I called that helper "the doula."

As my research continued, I began to notice that in America, when a mother has no doula she tends to become tense and anxious. Two now well-known research efforts had demonstrated how tension can interfere with the ejection reflex, which releases milk from the cells where it is stored into cavities in the mammary gland so that the baby can suck it out. When this reflex (also called the let-down) fails, so does lactation. An animal researcher demonstrated the effect by putting a cat on the back of a milking cow. He reported that the startled animal's milk stopped flowing (Ely and Peterson 1941). Another reseacher, a psychologist, experimented on herself. Over a period of several days, while she was nursing with her feet propped on a footstool, at random and without warning, her husband would pull the stool away, dumping her feet into icy water (Newton 1965). They weighed the baby before and after each feeding to measure how much milk he had ingested. Clearly during stressful nursing episodes the ejection reflex was inhibited and there was less milk.

So, I reasoned, in order to breastfeed the mother must be relatively free from stress, a state induced most effectively with the help of one or more supportive individuals. I was convinced I had the answers to why breastfeeding succeeded or failed, and I made sure there was a doula of some sort available from then on for myself and anyone else I could influence. Sure enough, all of us were able to breastfeed.

Working with thousands of new mothers over the years has convinced me that there is no time in the life of a woman more dramatic than when she has her first child and *first becomes a mother*. (And one can say that about many first-time fathers as well.) Changing from a woman to a mother, from someone with responsibility only for self, to a person responsible for the life of another human being, has no equal in any other life experience. This is the period I called *matrescence* (*patrescence* for males) (Raphael 1966). The first time is usually the most jarring and whether a woman describes it as wonderful or as traumatic, it is certain to be emotionally very powerful.

I have noted that most rituals and rites performed around childbirth are more conscientiously practiced for the first live child of a couple. Any subsequent births, even when the mother has finally given birth to a child of the culturally desirable sex, do not have the same impact. For the most part, these customs appear to help the woman go through the matrescent stage. We can expect that getting breastfeeding started, especially for the first time, depends on the kind of support implicit in these ceremonies.

The more I learned about lactation, the more astonished I was at how few studies had been done. Despite the critical place of lactation in the lives of all mammals, concern and research on childbirth apparently preceded an interest in breastfeeding by several generations. I began to fill in some gaps myself. I reviewed the patterns of interaction around the mother in twenty different mammalian species, did attitude-opinion interviews with 100 men and women in the United States and an equal number in England, as well as intensive, four-hour interviews with several dozen American, English and Japanese women. It seemed reasonable that breastfeeding was sufficiently important to make it the subject for a doctoral dissertation. But when I proposed it, a shock wave reverberated throughout the Columbia University anthropology department. It was a hard topic to sell in those days. Nobody was especially interested in it, and my professors were confused. Was breastfeeding anthropology? "Certainly," said Margaret Mead. Only one other anthropologist was convinced, Ray Birdwhistell. With his usual humor, he gave the subject some status by dubbing it, "Soft-Parts Physical Anthropology." Today, of course, research on breastfeeding is legitimate and plentiful.

Back then in 1966, however, neither foundations nor universities were willing to fund studies on breastfeeding. It wasn't until 1975, almost ten years later, that a farsighted "angel" provided a grant to found a nonprofit organization to promote and do research on breastfeeding. That's how The Human Lactation Center came into existence. (The founders, besides myself, were Dick and Pat Jelliffe of the UCLA School of Public Health, Margaret Mead, and Lucy Waletzky, a psychiatrist and sympathetic friend.)

The Human Lactation Center was but a few months old when we took on the AID contract to conduct a study of breastfeeding. The very fact that we were inexperienced in administering a government grant turned out to be a boon, for had we been less naive we undoubtedly would have known the study couldn't be done, not in the time we had, nor with the money we'd been given. In our innocence we agreed to complete the research within a year.

Slowly, as the months passed we began to realize just how naive we had been. We were expected to search the literature, host an international conference, fund all the fieldwork and my trips around the world to consult with the anthropologists, and work with consultants to analyze global factors that affected infant feeding and infant mortality.

Luckily, most of us had lots of energy and enthusiasm or it would never have been accomplished. With the help of some fine fieldworkers and researchers, we managed to do everything we had set out to do, and more.

We did it through a combination of ingenuity and old-fashioned New England stinginess. It was ingenuity, of course, that produced the idea of asking anthropologists to piggyback our research on studies they were already planning. As for parsimony, it meant carrying one's own luggage, staying in cheap hotels, and setting up back-to-back appointments so that as much as possible was crammed into each visit. Bribes, called "tipping," were a constant aggravation almost everywhere in the developing world. Because I was trying to hold down expenses, I was often caught up in a test of wills. Room space in the hotel in Cairo, a seat in a crowded plane in India, even permission to enter the country in Nigeria, all depended on what economists would call "informal income." I soon learned there are but two options: Pay and accept each culture on its own terms, or stay home.

Despite money worries, that summer was an incredibly intense, creative, productive time, and I was able to spend some time at most of the field sites. Everywhere I went, the anthropologists received me generously. In south India, Rajalakshmi Misra put me up in her young son's bedroom. In Sardinia, Elizabeth Mathias offered me her own bed while she slept on the floor, and in Trinidad, the Moslem patriarch of the community gave me his bedroom. The partitioned walls did not reach the ceiling, so I woke at 4:00 A.M. each day to hear him chanting his morning prayers from the living room where he was camping on the sofa.

The time I spent in the field had the intensity of a shipboard romance. For the duration of each visit, nothing in the outside world seemed real or important. After spending all day together, the fieldworker and I would sit up talking for half the night, puzzling over everything from the different ways that local mothers soothed their babies to the factors that had come together to make us anthropologists.

I sensed that, though these women had agreed to do an overwhelming amount of work for very little money, they were finding the whole subject of infant feeding fascinating. Because they already knew the culture and the people intimately, they were able to do in three months what other researchers would have taken at least a year to accomplish.

As a rule anthropologists remain in the field studying "their group" for a year or more. Within that time they collect a mass of material covering as many aspects of the culture as possible. To have been able to spend the greater part of three months on the description and analysis of breastfeeding and weaning patterns alone was remarkable. Seldom have any anthropologists had the time to choose and cover in such depth one small element in the lives of the people they have come to know so well. Most of them were talking to the women for the first time about what these mothers considered their deepest concerns—how they kept their babies alive. This brought the fieldworkers even closer to them. In fact, for some, that particular summer changed the focus of their careers, even their lives.

An anthropologist's relationship to the people she is studying is unique. In some ways she becomes part of the community and yet, at the same time, she is an outsider. Elizabeth Mathias, for example, had spent many summers doing fieldwork in shepherd villages in Sardinia. Because she was still an outsider, she could have the kind of easy, joking relationship with the men of the village that they'd never dream of having with a Sardinian woman. Yet she knew the language and the village so well that she could pun with her friends and appreciate local jokes based on events that had happened there years before. Her feeling for "her people" was very strong and special.

The late Gene Weltfish, a perceptive fieldworker and a gentle woman, once pointed out in a letter to me that "our discipline is a love affair." She noted that the months or years you spend in the field, especially the first time, are as intense, as fulfilling, as anything you are ever likely to experience. "It's the only time in your life when you can have relationships with people as if you were a child again. You ask them questions, and because you are there to learn and not to pass judgment, they can open up to you as to no one else." When you are in the community, you are continually asking for favors and for people's time. However, just by being there you provide novelty and excitement; to some people you also offer an abiding friendship.

Of course, there are problems at times. Not everyone welcomes the fieldworker. In fact, these days when an anthropologist comes into a community, people are often wary, and they are certainly very much aware that this inquisitive stranger is well-fed and, by their standards, rich. It never ceases to surprise me how kind and generous they can be. With an empty stomach, I doubt I could be as benevolent. Some fieldworkers find that their own sense of guilt at being so healthy and well-fed, however irrational it may be, is even harder to deal with than the outright hostility of some members of the community.

Nevertheless, the hostility can throw you off balance, as I discovered while I was in Egypt that summer visiting the village where our research was conducted. I was accompanied by a local doctor and anthropologist, Soheir Sukkary, a strikingly handsome woman. Squatting outside one of the village huts, we talked most congenially for a time with a small group of mothers. Suddenly, one of them demanded, "Why don't you give us back the powdered milk? Your government has taken our milk away."

For a time they had been getting free nonfat dry milk, supplied by the United States under the Food for Peace program. The children were doing well, they said, and then the milk supply stopped. Knowing the way such programs work, I could guess what had happened. The United States, like other governments, gives away food when there's a surplus as a way to keep prices up at home. When the surplus is gone, our generosity ends. However, it wouldn't have helped the women to tell them that. Their children's lives were at stake, and there was nothing I could say.

One day we strayed into a new section of this large village. As we were making our way back to our car, a mob of about forty children followed us, crying "Baksheesh! Baksheesh!" demanding coins in shrill voices. They were led by one taller and older boy carrying on his shoulder a painfully thin child who looked like a corpse, for he was asleep with his head dangling. The children began to snatch at our clothing and camera straps. We were frightened and walked faster. Women stood in doorways of their huts, half in and half out, contemptuous, laughing, goading on the mob. These youngsters were skinny little things, and individually incapable of hurting anyone. But

like the crows in Alfred Hitchcock's film *The Birds*, all together they had the terrifying effect of a multitude of menac-
ing creatures. As I tried not to break into a run, I felt the panic
so well portrayed in that film. After an eternity of being poked,
pulled, and threatened by these thin, hungry little people, we
reached the car, scrambled in, and tugged the door closed even
as they snatched at it. As we drove off, they pelted the car with
rocks.

Fortunately, most of the problems I encountered that summer were not that heartbreaking. For instance, we had to face
the fact that my arrival in a village caused a disruption, even
a breach, between the fieldworker and her informants. My
presence reminded them that she was an outsider, for suddenly they heard her speaking a foreign language and sharing
things with me that left them out.

The anthropologists handled this intrusion in several different ways. Some simply didn't introduce me to special people,
their chief informants. Others were clearly a little anxious but
carried on as before. One woman sent me off by car two days
earlier than I had planned to leave, warning me that this was
the only ride out that would be available for some time. Talking about it later, we began to understand the dynamics of what
had happened. Since she had to translate whatever they said,
and worse, we often discussed the comment in a language they
could not understand; and, since she and I were constantly together which changed the rhythm of her life with them, she
began to be identified more with me than with them. Getting
me out of the village was her way of protecting her relationship with *her* people.

The HLC anthropologist in Jamaica was Ida Daum, a tiny
woman, slim and graceful, whose previous work had been concerned with the economic structure of the Rastafarian community in Kingston. The Rastas don't open up easily to out-
siders, and Ida, an American black, had been hard-pressed to
win acceptance among them. (Later, she married one of the
leaders of the community.) I certainly didn't want to undo what
she had accomplished. I spent time with Ida as an observer,
but once I got a feel for the culture, I got out of her way.

I was there in the field to answer questions especially about infant feeding practices—remember, many of them had no prior experience with these issues. I was also anxious to see how the field methods we had suggested were working out.

We had provided the fieldworkers with some basic information about breastfeeding in an original protocol. It was a fifty-page treatise that included an extensive discussion of the physiological, behavioral, and psychological aspects of lactation, along with dozens of suggestions on how to gather information on this hitherto neglected function. The protocol also showed the anthropologist how to connect what she already knew about mothering in that particular culture to the new information she was collecting about breastfeeding. For instance, we explained how she could relate past events in the histories of mothers that she had recorded over the preceding years to help explain why one mother fed her infant rice water while another in the same community fed bush tea. The ultimate question we hoped to answer was why one baby survived and another did not.

Since our anthropologists were pressed for time (they were following the university calendar with only the summer months available) the puzzle was how were they to gather a comprehensive volume of information about the beliefs and practices of breastfeeding in such a short period of time.

The protocol described one shortcut that turned out to be an excellent tool. Each fieldworker was to bring women together in small groups to discuss breastfeeding. We anticipated that in a group, as the women compared notes, exaggerations and distortions would quickly become obvious and the limits and boundaries of behavior patterns would surface.

Two of the researchers were finding it difficult to set up the group discussions. We had suggested that the assembled group contain from four to seven women of at least three generations (adolescent/mother/grandmother). During the discussion we requested the fieldworkers to be as nondirective as possible, letting the women in the group ask questions, volunteer information, and say what their priorities were. We encouraged the ethnographers to listen carefully to the questions the women asked them, for they could lead to rich insights. The discussions were also a way to cross-check the accuracy of the information the fieldworkers were getting from individuals.

However, when I arrived in India, Rajalakshmi Misra reported that women of different castes wouldn't mix in such a group, and that when older women were present the younger ones, out of deference, kept quiet and didn't contribute to the discussion. Judy Gussler, working in a tiny village in St. Kitts, West Indies, found that none of her women could think of more than one or two friends with whom they'd be comfortable discussing intimate subjects.

Yet, when I appeared on the scene and proposed a group meeting, women came forward eagerly. It didn't take us long to figure out what had prompted this sudden change. I was a novelty and the women came partly because they were curious about me. I could make requests in my ignorance of the cultural dos and don'ts that would not be acceptable coming from the anthropologist who had finally been accepted by the community and was no longer treated as a stranger. They assumed that she had the good sense not to invite women who disliked each other into the same house; that she knew better than to ask people from different "castes" to sit down together and discuss intimate subjects.

Some of the fieldworkers reported that the women of their community were reluctant to talk about intercourse; yet it was an important issue from our point of view because in most cultures babies are weaned as soon as the mother becomes pregnant. We needed to know how women prevent pregnancy. In previous generations, long stretches of breastfeeding could be related to longer inter-pregnancy intervals. If women were breastfeeding for shorter periods of time, it might result in less successful spacing of their children. I suggested to the fieldworkers that instead of asking the women what they do to avoid becoming pregnant, that they use the technique of asking what "other people" generally do. My reasoning: Most people would like to be helpful and are happy to offer honest responses but on the delicate subject of intercourse, they find it easier if they can talk about it in the third person.

Though it was the fieldworkers' intimate knowledge of their

communities that gave the study its depth and authority, the fact that I did *not* know most of the cultures well was also an advantage. Sometimes I was able to see things they'd missed because they were now too familiar with the details of daily existence. I remember that one day I sat in a hutment outside New Delhi with an American anthropologist, an Indian physician and three mothers, sipping tea and eating sweets. I listened while the others all agreed that in their community babies were given nothing but breastmilk for the first five or six months. Yet, as I watched, from time to time the mother of a two-month-old ever so casually took little bits of whatever she was eating and fed it to the baby. The fieldworker was so close to the mother, her friend, so busy chatting with her and taking notes on their conversation that she never noticed what was happening. Margaret Mead used to tell her students to take notes nonstop on the first day in the field. The senses adjust so quickly she explained, they would never again see, feel nor hear many aspects of the culture as clearly.

Sometimes, the fieldworkers and I were able to spot one another's personal biases. For instance, though we were usually very objective, we bemoaned the fact that in one community the young girls were wearing jeans and their mothers, jeans skirts. Only Grandma continued to wear the traditional floor length black dress. Though we knew at times such dresses were hot and uncomfortable, still, we sorely missed the old costumes. A preference for the good old ways is the bane of our discipline. Had we not become anthropologists because we enjoyed differences?

Many of the fieldworkers railed against modernization and industrialization, against the intrusion of rock music and Sony radios, but the remarkable thing is that few of these attitudes came through in their accounts of what actually happened, what their informants said and what they concluded in their analysis of why people behaved as they did. These accounts were factually descriptive, despite an occasional lapse into sentimentality—testimony to their rigorous anthropological training.

During the field visits I became aware of some of the incorrect assumptions Westerners and upper-class men and women in other countries held about women in poverty. Health professionals, in particular, need to beware. For instance, they often take it for granted that nonliterate women must also be unintelligent. How wrong, and I can give examples from my own experiences in Jamaica.

I talked to dozens of mothers in the city as well as the countryside. I also interviewed doctors, midwives and other health professionals, listening while they spoke of their frustration with inadequate facilities—sometimes no toilets nor running water and few drugs. Even more important, I heard their opinions and complaints about the women they treated and squirmed as I listened to the stereotypes they had of their patients.

Many of them condemned young, poor Jamaican teenagers, calling them immoral because they became pregnant while still unmarried. Yet premarital pregnancy is a major social pattern in southern America and throughout the West Indies, even while the ideal remains the Western image of a married couple with children. Complaints abounded that these teenage mothers were selfish and irresponsible because they did not choose to breastfeed for all of the baby's first year.

However, the nurses at one village clinic convinced me that these criticisms were unjustified and unrealistic. They argued that, like it or not, the young people had few options. The nurses—stout, seasoned, down-to-earth women of around thirty—spoke realistically about breastfeeding, without sentimentality and without passing judgment. They explained that in Jamaica the mother's mother often looked after the baby while the mother earned the money to support the family. Though the new mother was generally unskilled, she could find a job because she was younger and employers could hire her for less money. From the Jamaican point of view, the older woman actually had the better deal. She could stay home, play with the baby, and clean her own house rather than go to work, as her daughter did, cleaning the homes of others. It's hardly surprising that for many young mothers, out most of the day, bottle-feeding was the only practical solution.

Typically, the young woman will leave her mother's home at the birth of her second child or during the second pregnancy and move into a tiny apartment with her current partner, perhaps leaving her firstborn with her mother. Even if she takes the baby with her, she generally finds it difficult to breastfeed. Her boyfriend, willing as he might be to support her and another man's baby, would want her to be available, free to go out with him, even if all they do is hold hands and walk down the street. Usually, they don't have enough money to do much else.

Unlike physicians with whom I talked—quick to damn the men for getting their women pregnant and then deserting them—the nurses emphasized that Jamaican fathers were not necessarily irresponsible or uncaring. Like the girls, they usually had their first child while still in their teens, and with no job and little chance of finding one, no way existed for them to support a family. However, the boy's mother often helped out in one way or another. He might not come around to the hospital to see the baby after it was born, but through friends he would keep in touch with how mother and child were doing.

One day while I was visiting Jubilee Hospital in Kingston, I left the building with a young woman I had interviewed earlier. As we walked out the front door of the hospital, she poked me with her elbow. "See behind the tobacco sign," she said. "That's my man." She whispered, "He's proud to be a father." Young men gain acceptance and are viewed as adults once they have children. But unable to support his child or move into a house of his own, he just hangs around in this manner.

The father may just linger nearby in the beginning, but after a while he generally begins to visit his child, often bringing the most meaningful gift he can afford—a large tin of powdered formula. Later, he will help as best he can by providing money to feed and clothe the youngster. However, if, as time passes, he fathers more children by this woman, then, as one of the nurses put it, "Whatever he give her, it is not enough; it can't be stretched . . . so he start the rejection thing but it is because he feels the role (of father) too big . . . (but) even if he has absconded, he is concerned." In fact, as the years pass, the man's relationships with his children become the most meaningful attachments in his life.

The nurses found little in the Jamaican experience that had

to do with the much-discussed decline of breastfeeding. They disagreed with the popular theory that poor, uneducated women in underdeveloped countries tend to model their lives on the lifestyle of middle- and upper-class women, a consequence of which is that when the richer classes give up breastfeeding, the poor soon follow their example. At least not in Jamaica. One nurse explained, "I being me has a lot to do with how I breastfeeding." As she put it, her choices as to how she feeds her child are a product of her particular needs and her situation. A young woman working for a woman whose baby was bottle-fed, might also give her own baby tinned or formula milk, "imitating" her employer not out of admiration or blind ignorance but because she saw a feeding pattern that worked and suited her own situation. Both women may bottle-feed; the more affluent mother because she chooses to go back to school, the poor mother because she has to work.

Eventually I realized how strong a belief persists that if a baby is malnourished, it must be because the mother (herself so poor) did something wrong. To my astonishment, I heard health professionals blaming the victims. I firmly believe we do wrong to suggest that uneducated women are not as intelligent as we are or that they love their babies less than we do. Each mother does the very best for her baby. Besides, ultimately that child's appearance, accomplishments, and state of health reflect on her. We often forget that other people's reactions to the child affect the mother's self-image.

I'll not forget one particular conversation I had with a young Jamaican mother. I asked her how much water she added when she made up the baby's formula. I suspected she diluted the formula so that the baby wasn't getting sufficient nutrition. She sensed my unspoken criticism and retorted sharply, "I maybe no read, but I no blind." Even if she couldn't read the label, she knew how the milk should be made up. Obviously, she couldn't afford *not* to dilute it. How unreasonable for anyone to have thought she didn't know what she was doing. You can't feed a baby eight, ten times per day for weeks without knowing a lot about his needs, his appetite, his preferences, and the quality of milk that will meet those needs.

I spent some time in clinic waiting rooms with mothers and

their babies. Caught in a health program that was under-
staffed, indifferent and highly routinized, the women had to
devise ingenious ways to get around the system. At one clinic
a number of mothers were sitting in a row lined up against
the wall in a hallway, each holding a baby in her lap. I watched
while one woman in the line quietly passed a handsome baby
bonnet and sweater to someone farther up the row, who was
waiting her turn to see the doctor. I found out what was going
on. If a baby was not nicely dressed, the medical staff was not
polite; so the mother with the better looking baby clothes was
sharing them with others.

A few minutes later I heard one woman ask another, "What's
wrong with your baby?" The second woman described the infant's symptoms—he had a serious respiratory infection. She
also explained her own dilemma: She had to get back to work
the next day or she would be fired. The two of them discussed
the situation and soon agreed that she should move farther
back in the line, so that her turn wouldn't come until after noon.
They knew the doctors changed shifts at noon and the afternoon doctor was more likely to prescribe penicillin than the
morning doctor, who was more conservative about handing out
the drugs the government supplied free to the poor. Both
women believed that with one shot of penicillin the baby would
be in good enough shape, with his fever reduced, so that he
could be left at the day care nursery the next day.

Another insight about how uninformed we are about the
motivations of women came to me one day when I was sitting
in a tiny two-room house in a village outside Kingston with a
twenty-one-year-old mother who cradled a beautiful, healthy,
six-month-old baby in her arms. Two beds had been squeezed
into the adjoining tiny, spotlessly clean room. We sat on the
two chairs butted against a small table with a plastic top and
squeezed in between another bed and a stove. I asked whether
she was going to breastfeed another six months. No, indeed.
The young woman's eyes sparkled with anticipation as she described her plans for the future. "I'm going to go to Montego
Bay," she told me. "I'm going to leave my baby with my mother
there and I'm going to work in a hotel. Soon I'll buy a new
dress. Then I'm going to stand by the gate on Sunday and watch

1. Egyptian village women talk with Dana Raphael and Soheir Sukkary about breastfeeding and weaning practices. "We breastfeed; we are not city women."

2. Rajalakshami Misra, the Indian anthropologist, reported that village mothers had a great distrust of the health care system. "To put it in a crude way, when the baby is unable to move its limbs then the mother feels she must get medical help."

3. Elizabeth Mathias records the rituals and practices of slaughtering a goat for a holy feast. Because she was foreign she could joke with the men as local unmarried women could not.

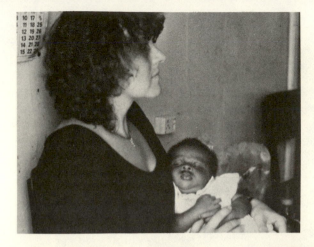

4. Judy Gussler holds the baby of one of her best informants during a lengthy discussion about why Kittitian women want to immigrate. "Most of these women have one leg in St. Kitts and the other on the way to the islands or the United States. There are so few jobs here and their lives are not interesting."

5. Right to left around the table, anthropologists Ida Daum, Marion Zeitlin, Lee Stapleton, Carol Bryandt and Judy Gussler compare notes about fieldwork during a weekend conference at the end of the project.

6. Margaret Mead and the author discussing the contents of the final report of the project in her impossible to find "tower" office at the American Museum of Natural History. Her spirit envelops this book. Courtesy of Frank White © 1976.

the people go by." I was stunned by the contrast between her idea of excitement and mine—her feelings about breastfeeding and mine.

That summer, as I became increasingly aware of the context of breastfeeding, of the way it fits into the lives of millions of women, there was a gradual but profound change in my thinking. I began to see breastfeeding as many Third World women saw it—perhaps pleasurable but certainly quite ordinary. In the Western world many of us turn to breastfeeding as a little gem: as a divine opening up of emotional contact, as something important that we can do with our bodies and not be ashamed, as a way of validating our womanliness. And furthermore, finally in the 1980s, especially in the United States, everybody makes a fuss of approval over the mother who does breastfeed.

Most poor women live in places that are grim, sparse, relatively clean, but seldom what we would consider sanitary. Their lives are repetitive, stultifying and full of stress; for many, one day is often exactly like every other day. Their excitements are limited to a trip to town or a chance to take in a movie. Sure they care about their babies, but, to them, breastfeeding is a run-of-the-mill necessity and sometimes something that interferes with their chance to improve their days and better the lives of their children.

That extraordinary summer finally ended and the anthropologists sent in their field notes together with reports on the economy of the country they'd studied, on the history and ethnography of their particular community, and on the health status of mothers and children.

In December 1976, we invited all the fieldworkers to come to the center for a weekend get-together. It was billed as the Wall-to-Wall Anthropologists' Conference because we had first planned, with financial constraints, to put everyone up in sleeping bags on the carpets of the center. Luckily, we did manage rooms at a motel. The idea was that we would share with each other the work we had done and prepare for a presentation of our research findings at an international conference scheduled for the spring.

Before the meeting all of us at the center were high with anticipation. We organized and planned every detail to get the most from the conference and make our guests comfortable despite a tight budget. But the weekend was a disaster. All the good will, the warmth, sharing and professionalism degenerated into a sour, bitter contest of wills. Instead of a celebration, it was a wake. For months afterward we kept asking, "What happened?"

We brought together a group of high-powered women who had never met before. They had done some extraordinary and stimulating research that summer. They had produced reams of original material. As enormously rewarding as it was, they had also been grossly underpaid and overworked.

Besides, as with most anthropologists, they were possessive of "their material" and "their people." Much later, one of the group, who was by then a good friend, suggested an interesting psychological premise: She speculated that one reason for the breakdown of the meeting might have been a genuine grief the fieldworkers felt at having lost control of their material, the treasures they'd so painstakingly collected. To them, it was not just data but a piece of their lives, the product of a very intense and intimate relationship with people whom they had learned to love. One of them admitted later that exposing her material to all of us had suddenly brought her to grips with a latent fear that what we might write could possibly damage her relationship with her people. According to our contract, the center had the obligation to write this very book, but it was little comfort to her that she still could use her own research as she wished.

Surely, some must have come expecting recognition for the marvelous job they'd done and plenty of time for sharing. Instead, after dinner that first night we immediately began videotaping them, for we'd planned to use the tapes to help disseminate the information they had gathered. The next day we divided into small groups for discussions; each group was provided with an agenda and requested to come up with some recommendations as to some steps AID could take to increase breastfeeding and reduce malnutrition.

At dinner Saturday night I suggested eagerly we could all

do another study together on lactation and the way it functions (or fails to) as a natural contraceptive. That landed like a bombshell. Suddenly, two of the anthropologists reacted vociferously. They said they were not going to invade the privacy of the women in their cultures by revealing such intimate information. Sarcastically, one asked if we wanted to see the birth rate reduced in those cultures for racist reasons.

At any rate, the conference, so amicably begun on Friday, dissolved on Sunday in anger and misunderstanding. What had been a "high" of intellectual and personal sharing became a low of distrust. That weekend was confusing to us all and it was one of the most painful of my life.

Over the next few months the center's staff thought and talked a lot about the dynamics of the weekend, trying to analyze what had happened. One day, during a meeting with other groups we met a "facilitator," a woman who was a specialist in group dynamics, and we learned from her that it was not unusual for such a meeting to end unexpectedly in acrimony. Apparently, when a group of very intense people meet in close quarters, sometimes any small thing can trigger a clash and then the situation spins out of control. Experienced conference organizers we were told, are prepared for such a crisis and almost always have a trained facilitator available to assume control and get the group back together. Nonetheless, the experience, understood or not, still left scars.

As we continued to work with the raw material the study had produced, many of our ideas were gradually changing. As I've already mentioned, a year earlier when the study began we had expected to confirm certain assumptions: Breastfeeding was declining; as a result, more babies were dying; and the multinational companies' aggressive marketing of their products in the developing countries was responsible.

Yet, in the cultures we studied, much to our surprise, a decline was not a major part of the problem. In some, breastfeeding was still universal. In others, if there was a "decline," it was not in the practice of breastfeeding but rather in *the number of months of breastfeeding*. Furthermore, the very poor seldom used processed milk to bottle-feed their babies. The simple reason: They couldn't afford it. The one exception were the women who participated in a WIC (Women, Infants, and Children) program in Houston, where the milk for infants of the very poor was provided without cost.

Most important, we learned that mixed feeding was common. Babies were breastfed but they were given other foods as well from a very early age. At first, we wondered if this was a coincidence, or did the desperately poor, uneducated mothers actually know more than the Western doctors who maintained that breastmilk was all a baby needed for most of the first year of life.

Was it possible that the particular cultures we had studied systematically were atypical, that elsewhere in the world breastfeeding was threatened in the way we had anticipated? Not so. A WHO/UNICEF two-year Collaborative Study on Breast-feeding (1979), a survey of 22,857 women in nine countries, revealed these same patterns. Unfortunately, no statistical reliability can be offered to support their findings, but the clinical data from the nine-country survey did at least reveal that one-third of the lactating mothers used supplemental food on a regular basis by the end of three months.

In hindsight, the information gained through intimate, one-to-one relationships and careful, in-community study (the trademark of anthropological research) remain for us, even today, the best methods we have of discovering not only *how* the process of breastfeeding works but *why* women do what they do. The patterns we found are not intended to be statistically valid, but unobtrusive measures based on cross-cultural insights and rigid protocols for observation and interviewing, still benchmarks of anthropological research. The methods proved themselves reliable as we began to compare cultures and analyze the data.

The women's stories described in this book offer the reader a chance to consider some of the evidence that led us to our conclusions.

When I began the HLC study, I had a fairly simple goal in mind: *Ask* women about breastfeeding and let them speak for themselves. Through this book, I hope to give these women a chance to speak for themselves again.

2

SAGADA, THE PHILIPPINES

Odani lives in Sagada, an Igorot* village in the mountain region of northern Luzon in the Philippines. She has borne eight children, and five are still living. She's a stocky woman, barely five feet tall, with a pretty face already seamed with age, though at the time of the study she was just 34 years old. She and her husband shared a one-room, thatched-roof house (called *agagamang*) with their three youngest children who were then 3, 5, and 10. Odani's 13-year-old daughter was living with an aunt while her 15-year-old son, who had left high school to help support the family, lived on the farm where he worked.

Odani's day begins at 4:30 A.M. when she gets up to set sweet potato vines boiling in a rusty kerosene tin—breakfast for the family's pigs. Her stove is simply three large stones placed on the dirt floor in the center of the room. A wood fire is built under them, and the kerosene tin sits on top. Since the house has no windows or chimney, the air soon grows thick with smoke, but Odani is used to that.

As soon as the vines have cooked, Odani carries them outside and throws them in a stone trough for the pigs that live in sunken pits just a few feet from the door of the house. Then she prepares the family breakfast of boiled camotes—dry, mealy, sweet potatoes. Since her house has no running water,

*The designation I-gorot (of the mountains) is used in a general sense to describe the language and residents of the region. It has no ethnic significance.

she sends one of her older children to fetch some from an out-
door tap, one of several that supply the village. It's a ten-min-
ute walk, there and back.

When her household is in order, Odani sets out in the pen-
etrating cold of the dawn for her fields, where she grows vegetables and rice for her family. At that hour it is still very chilly
(in the fifties) and when it rains, it may never get much
warmer. However, on fine days it can get very hot once the
sun burns away the morning mist that clings to the steep green
mountainside. While Odani is away, her children are at school
or they are looked after by neighbors and relatives in the *da-
pay*, the house for the young unmarried men, or the equivalent for young women, the *ebgan*.

Odani wears a wrap-around skirt made of a fabric she wove
herself. Most of her clothes are dark blue, since blue is the
cheapest yarn sold at the local store. The skirt is topped with
a cotton shirt she bought for a nickel, picking it out from the
bales of used clothing for sale in the market. She has twisted
her long, black hair up out of the way at the back of her head,
and she is barefoot. The soles of her feet are deeply calloused
from a lifetime of walking without shoes; sometimes in wet
weather they develop deep cracks.

A small, handwoven basket hangs from the belt Odani wears
at her waist. As she works in the fields, she will pick up snails,
crickets, and crabs and store them in the basket to "sweeten"
the evening family pot. She will fill a much larger basket with
crops, which she will carry home balanced on her head.

Odani works her fields with a digging stick tipped with a
hand-forged iron spatula. Besides the 8 to 10 hours she will
spend planting, weeding, or picking vegetables, she must tramp
up and down the mountainside because, like many people in
Sagada, she has rice fields in several different places. These
terraced fields were passed down in her family, becoming
smaller and smaller with successive generations as the family
increased and each plot of land was divided among the children.

Because Odani comes from one of the poorer families in Sagada, her little parcels of land grow only enough rice to feed
her family for about one month out of every year. Most of their

income is spent buying rice, the staple grain for that area. It is the most highly regarded food and the mainstay of the Igorot diet, except for the very poor who must make do with camote. Odani also grows vegetables in a "swidden," a farm plot originally cleared by the slash-and-burn method.

By afternoon when Odani leaves the fields she has filled her basket with camotes, vines, vegetables, and rice. On some days the basket weighs as much as 40 or 50 pounds, and she may carry it six or eight miles.

Once home, she sets to work to cook more pig food, pound the rice with mortar and pestle, peel and cook camote, or prepare vegetables. The evening meal may consist of plain boiled rice, rice served with squash or leafy vegetables, or (a favorite recipe among the poor) rice and camote boiled together. When the whole family is home, she needs eight cups of raw rice to make a meal. Of course, there's also laundry to wash (in cold water without soap), weaving to do, and the children to tend.

Odani's husband shares the housework and gathers the firewood from the mountainside on communal land, available to everyone in the village. In this culture, where there is an equitable division of household tasks, wood gathering is traditionally done by men and boys. However, Odani's husband hires himself out as a laborer or carpenter's assistant by the day or by the week, so when he is away from home she gathers the wood herself. This means she collects branches that have fallen or trims them off the trees; using vines, she wraps the wood into a huge bundle and balances it on her head. It is heavy work and almost a daily chore, so when she cooks she uses as little wood as possible.

Odani's house has no electricity, and in the evening the only light comes from the cooking fire. To bathe, she goes to one of the community taps and discreetly scrubs herself under the cold water with a smooth stone—soap is a luxury. Most people bathe in public this way, and passersby politely avert their eyes.

Odani's 18-hour day ends sometime around 9:00 P.M. Every day she labors in the fields, cooks for her family, washes and cleans, and yet she has breastfed *all* her children.

And that was what The Human Lactation Center study was about; we wanted to learn: How did she manage?

Lee Stapleton, the anthropologist who returned to Sagada for the study, had lived there from 1960 to 1970, while her husband, an Episcopal priest, ran a high school for Igorot young people. Lee was in her early 20s at that time and had three children, an infant, a 2-year-old and a 4-year-old; two more babies were born during her 10-year stay.

In 1976, excited to see the village and old friends again, she arrived in Sagada in August at the height of the monsoon season, which starts in April and lasts through mid-October. In August 1976, the village had about 100 inches of rain. "That year we all got very wet and cold," she recalled.

Sagada has a population of about 3,000 in the village itself, with about 7,000 more people living in outlying hamlets. It is tucked in a high valley in an isolated part of the mountains, at an altitude of about 5,000 feet.

Because of the mountainous terrain, villages in the area have always been isolated from one another. One can travel on foot for three hours and come upon a group that speaks a different language, and as recently as 60 to 75 years ago practiced warfare and head-hunting. One of the older women Lee knew in Sagada recalled that when she was a child, "they were very fond of telling us to eat with both feet on the floor so that if the *boso* (head-takers) came you could flee . . . . Whenever we heard shouts in the night we felt fear." Accounts written by the early Spanish settlers are full of references to the "remote and inclement heights" inhabited by the *Igorrotes*, who recognized no authority except their own chieftains and reared their children in "abject liberty."

The road that connects Sagada to the outside world is extremely rough, made of dirt topped with rocks chopped up by the road crews. Fortunately for the villagers at least a stretch of asphalt runs from one end of the village to the other. In 1976, the residents of Sagada owned about 20 cars and trucks, a means of livelihood for local entrepreneurs who hire them out to transport people and freight to the outlying hamlets or the provincial capital.

For a change, it was sunny and warm one Sunday morning when Lee recorded a visit to Odani and their talk about rearing and feeding children. In Sagada the more Westernized

7. Although 30 percent of Igorot women in the Philippines attain a college education, they are still committed to the old ways. For instance, tattoos are still considered a sign of beauty.

8. A woman weaves in the traditional fashion in front of her home overlooking exquisitely terraced rice fields. Igorot houses are small, with very low ceilings. Once inside, one must stoop, so many activities are performed out-of-doors.

families live in shiny metal houses along the asphalt road, but the less acculturated poor, like Odani, live in the *ili*, the old part of the community, back from the road. The houses there are the traditional Igorot one-room structures, built of hand-hewn timber and topped with a steep thatched roof. The timber walls are only waist-high, enclosing about ten square feet of living space, and the thatch, which has a generous over-hang, reaches almost to the ground. The only opening is a single, low door, and a visitor has to bend almost double to enter the house, and once inside can't stand up straight. "The people spend a lot of their lives bent over," Lee said. "They stoop both at home and as they work in the fields."

Odani's dooryard was paved with stones and on either side, just six feet from the door, were the two sunken pigpens, lined with stones, each with one pig. The smell of excrement was pervasive since the manure-filled pigpens were used by this family, like most in the *ili*, as latrines.

The house had no furniture, only implements: cooking vessels, a mortar and pestle, a few simple farm tools, basket containers and basket plates, bowls made from coconut shells. The floor was partly board and partly dirt, and parents and children slept on smooth boards, slightly elevated, like low shelves. There were no mattresses and little bedding.

Odani had stayed home that day to talk to Lee, and, unaccustomed to sitting down at ten in the morning, she found it difficult to stay awake in spite of the two small children who, clamoring for her attention, climbed in and out of her lap. They pulled at their mother's clothing, played with her long hair, and made a lot of noise; yet she seldom scolded them, remaining patient and nurturant throughout.

Odani began by describing the birth of her first child. Among the Igorot most babies are born at home, with the husband or another relative acting as midwife. However, Odani's husband was away when her time came, and she was alone. Few women would want to be alone during childbirth, yet Odani's face was almost expressionless, and there was little display of emotion as she described the experience.

"My labor started early in the morning," she recalled, "and went on into the night; then the baby came out. The 'house' (afterbirth) followed maybe an hour later. I felt dizzy and afraid but I was ashamed to go to the hospital. I had no money to pay." She was 19 years old.

Odani cut the umbilical cord to match the length of her new son's leg, then coiled and bound it over his navel with a rag—the Igorot believe a long cord insures a long life. Following the Igorot custom, she gave the baby a bath in cold water and said a prayer over him, so that in later life he wouldn't be afraid to wash in cold water and wouldn't complain when he was cold. Very soon after, as is the custom, she put the baby to breast.

After Odani's husband had come home, he asked neighbors to send a messenger to tell the grandparents the baby had been born, and they came as quickly as they could, bringing salt-pork and rice, to say the traditional *kidlos* prayer: "May the breast milk flow freely, may the child live safely, and, like us, avoid all misfortune." For the next few days the house was out of bounds to all but the immediate family.

As expected, Odani had carried on with her usual workload right up to the time of birth, even when she felt nauseated, weak or dizzy. However, once she gave birth she became a *mensakot*, a new mother, and the change in her life was dramatic.

From the birth until the time the cord dropped off in about a week, she and her husband were expected to stop all outside work. The grandparents and sometimes other relatives and friends filled in, tending their fields and gathering food for the family. In fact, for the next two months it was assumed that Odani would do almost nothing other than take care of the baby. A complex of taboos specifically forbade many of her usual activities.

Ordinarily, during that first week after birth, the *mensakot*'s mother visits daily to help the new father do the household chores. She also gives her daughter daily sponge baths with warm water in which guava leaves have been steeped. Since Odani's mother died when she was a child, it was her mother-in-law who came to help with the housework, and her husband gave her the herbal baths. (It is not common but men can perform some traditionally female roles. Another young mother told Lee that her father taught her a lot about breastfeeding, and a woman who usually had her babies in the local hospital said she preferred to have her father with her during the delivery because he was more of a comfort than either her husband or her mother.)

After the umbilical cord dropped off, Odani's relatives assembled once again to kill and eat a chicken, officially name the child, and share in other rituals. Because meat is scarce and expensive, the Igorot usually eat it only on ceremonial occasions. Normally, the baby's father buries the umbilical cord and says a prayer over it, but Odani chose to perform this ritual herself. If her husband played the traditional part in all the customs and rites surrounding birth, he would be charged with keeping all the taboos as well. It would be very risky then for him to break the taboos that prohibit new fathers from building stone walls, or driving nails before the baby has cut its first teeth at six to eight months of age. Since Odani's husband was a carpenter, if he observed the taboos he wouldn't be able to earn a living. Like many young village men today, he skirted some traditions; but if the baby became sick, he would almost certainly worry and wonder whether he was to blame.

For two months relatives tended Odani's fields for her so that she could devote herself to her infant. All families provide such an interlude if they possibly can. Igorot women say that at such times they feel serene and have a sense of well-being and personal worth. The custom, which is fairly universal in traditional cultures, has survival value. The fact that the mother can devote herself entirely to the baby for two months, until lactation is firmly established, could make the difference between a dead infant and a living one.

Lee observed that the kind of attention a woman receives at such times is an intensification of the normal Igorot patterns of helping and sharing. "The supportive network including neighbors and friends is always there," she said. "Life for the Igorot is difficult but seldom lonely."

Symbolizing the dramatic change in her life that motherhood has brought about, the *mensakot* acquires a new name with the birth of her first child. Because Odani's baby was named "Domanay," henceforth she herself was known as "Inan

Domanay"—mother of Domanay. Her own name would rarely be used again. Similarly, her husband became "Aman Domanay," father of Domanay. (Anthropologists call this form of child-related address, "teknonymy.") Among the Igorot, children validate a marriage and are highly valued. In fact, a couple is not considered legally married until they have a baby.

Though people referred to Odani's new son as "Anak Odani," son of Odani, and used his mother's (or father's) name when speaking *about* him, in talking *to* him they generally used the name bestowed on him by his grandparents. In addition, *ili* children are given a Western name by the local priest or catechist, which they use later when they attend school.

Odani carried her baby with her everywhere, tucked into an *eban* or tight blanket-sling. She almost never put him down or allowed him to cry, and since the *eban* is worn across the front of the body, it was extremely easy for her to suckle her infant whenever he was hungry or restless. The baby slept with his parents at night.

As he grew bigger, she switched the *eban* to the back, an arrangement that made it easier for her to carry his weight and also gave him more freedom to look around and to reach out. In Sagada, children are carried in the *eban* by parents, grandparents and older siblings throughout their first year and often well into the second, though once they've learned to walk they're tied on less often. When sick, hurt, or frightened, a youngster often cries for the comfort of the *eban*, and Lee noted, "Igorot children may cry and expect to be tied on until they are old enough themselves to tie on a new baby."

Physiologically, a woman becomes a mother at the instant she gives birth to a living infant. However, socially and psychologically, becoming a mother is more complex. I call this process *matrescence*, and in different cultures it occurs at different points in time. Some societies begin to treat a woman as a mother the moment it's clear she's pregnant; in others she's not really a mother until she has given birth to an infant of the "right" (usually male) sex. Among the Igorot, motherhood coincides with the birth of a live child and is confirmed by the birth rituals that come immediately afterwards, but it takes a woman about two months after the birth to make the transition, to really be considered a mother.

During that time she gets support from family and friends, and she receives much mothering herself, usually from her own mother. As I explained in Chapter 1, I call the person who mothers the mother the "doula," and her (or sometimes his) presence and support are crucial if the mother is to succeed in breastfeeding her infant. In general, where mothers have a doula, they can breastfeed; where they don't, they have trouble. Among the Igorot and in other cultures where a mother *must* breastfeed if her infant is to survive, the family will usually manage to provide a doula (as one person or several part-time supportive persons) unless they are destitute or there are no kin particularly interested in making an investment in that child.

Like most Igorot women who farm, Odani had to go back to her fields when the baby was two months old. She couldn't take him along since the fields were so far away and her load coming back was so heavy. At first she went only for short periods, leaving her son with his grandmother. If he cried because he was hungry while she was gone, he was given tea or water, skimmed from a pot of boiling rice, to tide him over.

This was the beginning of his weaning. The dictionary defines "to wean" as "to cause (a child or young animal) to become accustomed gradually to food other than its mother's milk." Unfortunately, many people assume instead that weaning occurs when the mother decides to *stop* breastfeeding—and there may be nothing gradual about that. Or it is used to describe a baby who is changed from the breast to a bottle or from a bottle to solid foods. In fact, the word "weaning" proved to be very complex, and we redefined it several times during the HLC study. We are now convinced that—as Margaret Mead once told me—"Weaning is always." In every culture in the study, mothers introduced foods other than breastmilk when the baby was very small, offering them in gradually increasing amounts. Eventually, we decided to abandon the word for descriptions which spelled out the process exactly as it was being practiced in each case.

Sometimes when Odani was in the fields her breasts would tingle as the ejection reflex occurred. The sensation meant milk was being released from the alveoli, the cavities in the breast where it was stored, into the ducts leading to the nipples where it remains until the baby sucks it out. Igorot mothers believe this is a sign that, miles away, the baby is hungry and crying, so if they possibly can, they hurry home.

At home, carried in the blanket sling, Odani's infant was offered the breast whenever he awoke. She went right on stirring the pot or shelling beans as she fed him. At night he slept beside her, and if he woke up hungry, they snuggled together and he nursed. Gradually, Odani spent longer and longer periods in the fields until, by the baby's fourth month, she was working all day again. Now the baby needed more food, so he was offered watery rice porridge and sugared tea.

Occasionally, while an Igorot mother is away, another mother will feed the baby for her. "We know the milk from another mother's breast is as clean and good as ours," one woman explained to Lee. Though a neighbor might help out once in awhile, only a close relative would be asked to do so on a regular basis. Most mothers believe it's important that the substitute mother have a baby of approximately the same age. They're convinced breastmilk changes as the baby grows older, becoming unsuitable for a younger infant. Years earlier, Margaret Mead reported that the Arapesh assume that with time the milk changes. Today, preliminary tests are beginning to back up this belief. Margaret Mead even suggested that we may have many "milk types," just as we have blood types.

Breastfeeding was not always pleasant for Odani. "Sometimes it is so painful when the baby sucks," she said, "but one has to be patient." Many women mentioned to Lee how much pain they experienced from sore or cracked nipples. When a *mensakot* has such difficulty, her mother is usually there, or her father or husband, to give advice and encourage her to tolerate the discomfort.

The Igorot believe that when a woman comes home from the fields, she should bathe her breasts in cool water because a baby who drinks from a warm breast may develop diarrhea. They don't expect hard work to affect the mother's milk supply, nor do they feel that breastfeeding should be tiring for a woman. If a baby refuses to suck or appears too weak to suck, they don't automatically assume that there is something wrong with the baby. They believe it's a sign of trouble or misunderstanding between husband and wife. At these times, they call in a dream interpreter to tell them what to do, and if they follow the interpreter's prescription, they expect a change in the baby's feeding behavior.

"It seems worth noting," Lee said, "that in Igorot there's just one word, *soso*, for breast, nipple, breastmilk, and breastfeeding." The breasts are strictly identified with the act of breastfeeding, unlike Western cultures, where the female breast has both cosmetic and feeding connotations.

The Igorot assume that what the mother eats is passed on to the baby. In fact, there is a myth about how this fact was first discovered. One of the women recounted the tale for Lee:

There is a story they always tell of the couple from Bogang who had two gantas (the equivalent of 24 measuring cups) of rice that they set aside because they had a new baby. They were waiting, it is said, until the baby knew how to eat. Now, one day the mother went to the forest, and as she went, she picked and ate *sabsabbeng* (a red berry). After she got home, she fed the child from her breasts. And when he moved his bowels, the feces were red. So the husband asked, "Did you feed the child something red?" and his wife said, "No, I just ate some berries myself." And the husband said, "Ah, so that is how it is! Now we can eat the rice we have been saving, because, as you see, it will also be eaten by the child." And it is said this is how we came to do the thing that we always do now: Whenever we kill a chicken or offer salt-pork, we give the child's share to the mother.

In keeping with this belief, on ceremonial occasions mothers are given a little extra food to acknowledge their infants as new members of the group. In the process, all this activity and attention serves to make the new mother feel special and in that way supports her. The custom of offering a mother her baby's share of the ceremonial meat, like the taboos that prevent a *mensakot* from returning to the fields immediately, helps to meet the needs of the mother and to facilitate breastfeeding.

In Sagada pregnant and lactating women, and growing children, are all expected to be *men-sewe-seweng*, constantly hungry. Many mothers say their daily consumption of rice increases while they're breastfeeding by half a cup to a cup of raw rice daily, and, like their children, they snack on cold boiled camotes between meals.

Odani's diet, however, changed very little, since she couldn't afford extra food. She did try to have more vegetables when they were available, and she put plenty of *labay*—the cooking water from the vegetable pot—on her rice. She also drank *sabeng* at times, since it was supposed to be good for breastfeeding mothers. *Sabeng* is a potent, fermented brew of rice water, camote and vegetable parings and millet.

Like other Igorot mothers, Odani remembered the months when her baby was teething as a difficult and dangerous period. "Children always get sick at this time," she said. Most often, they develop diarrhea, a fever, or both, and sometimes they are not able to tolerate any foods except breastmilk. In most of the cultures included in the HLC study, mothers singled out teething as a time when babies are apt to become sick.

Certainly, the teething itself doesn't *cause* the illness; rather, the child is irritated, upset, physically stressed and is using up precious energy. The malnourished child becomes vulnerable.

When Odani's babies were teething at seven months, and she had to stop breastfeeding because she was pregnant, it was hard. "I do not like to wean at this time," she said. "I pity them because they are already sick, but when I know I am pregnant, I wean them." The Igorot believe that after a mother becomes pregnant, her milk turns oily and difficult to digest and may give the nursing infant diarrhea. In fact, the women say that sometimes the first sign of pregnancy is diarrhea in the breastfed baby. However, many mothers, continue to breastfeed despite their fears for the child—some, because they have no other choice.

A woman's metabolic system functions with great efficiency during pregnancy and for the first few months of lactation. However, efficiency may not be enough. If she's undernourished to begin with, the combination of pregnancy and breastfeeding could undermine her health still more. Equally important, the new baby is far more likely to be underweight at birth and thus weaker to begin with. The belief that a pregnant woman should not breastfeed may serve to protect both mother and child in societies such as Sagada, where many adults have an "unbalanced" diet or simply don't get enough to eat.

Though many of the Igorot mothers told Lee they stopped breastfeeding because the baby was eating other foods and they felt breastmilk was no longer necessary, their most frequent explanation was the onset of another pregnancy—as it is throughout the world.

Breastfeeding has a contraceptive effect. It inhibits ovulation for nine months on the average (Huffman 1977). No individual woman, however, can be *certain* that breastfeeding will protect her for that period of time. Many factors intervene. For instance, the physical condition of the mother makes a difference; a well-nourished woman is apt to resume menstruation and become fertile sooner than an undernourished woman (Frisch 1978).

Women all over the world are well aware that breastfeeding does delay the next pregnancy, though they too joke about exceptions. An American anthropologist, Michele Shedlin, working in Mexico, once commented on how closely spaced her own children were—they were then six, eight, and nine. "Of course," her Mexican village friend reminded her, "You didn't breastfeed."

Most Igorot mothers said they prefer to breastfeed until their babies are at least a year old. Odani breastfed her fifth child, a son, for a year and a half. "He was walking and he was still not weaned," she recalled. "He had many teeth, and that is why I was finally forced to wean him. But it was difficult. That is when I had to put hot pepper on my breasts, and even that did not discourage him. It took a long time to wean this one." Other mothers told of applying ginger or chili-pepper sauce to their nipples to discourage a child who still wanted the breast.

It has been my own observation that when a baby resists the end of breastfeeding, it is likely to be because the mother is inexperienced and handles the transition poorly, or because the child is picking up—and reacting to—the ambivalence in the mother. Many women experience a deep sense of loss when it's time to give up that close contact with the baby. On the other hand, in Sagada, the expectation is that breastfeeding will terminate suddenly despite the shock and distress in the child.

Odani's children were often very ill when they were infants. Lee felt that in Sagada today children get sick about as often as they ever did, but they're more likely to survive childhood illnesses because there is a hospital and available medication nearby. Just a generation or two ago, most mothers lost several children. Odani and her family are still vulnerable, as was her grandmother, because the family can't afford sufficient medical care.

Odani's second child, a boy, was sick almost from the time he was born and died when he was six months old. Her third, a girl, was very sick as an infant, too; in desperation, Odani took her to the local clinic, where the staff said she needed vitamins. Odani got the money to pay for them, and the child survived. Her fourth baby died at the age of seven months.

"There's always one 'in-between' who dies," she told Lee. "The first lives, the second dies, the third lives, the fourth dies, the fifth lives. These," she said, indicating the two children in her lap, "are the only ones without an 'in-between.'"

Just a short time before, her eighth baby had been stillborn. "It was during the seventh month that blood started to come," she explained. "This is when I went to the clinic. They just said, 'Well, it must be about to come out.' And I thought, 'How can it be about to come out when it is only seven months?' All this time I felt so weak and the movement in my belly was weak, also . . . . It was night when my labor began . . . . When the baby came it did not cry, it didn't move. This was a hard time for me. I cut the umbilical cord . . . still the baby didn't move. The next morning I called my father and he buried the baby." The three children who died are buried under the paving stones in the front yard, because the Igorot believe that if a small child rests far from home and becomes lonely, he may call other children to join him.

Igorot children like Odani's are highly vulnerable for two reasons. First, the environment is severely contaminated despite the fact that the local water supply is clean and safe. For example, one day when Lee was talking to Odani, their conversation was interrupted twice when rats capsized a storage basket. And, as we mentioned, Odani, like everyone in the *ili*, keeps pigs. Pigs are a ready source of cash and are needed for a sacrifice when there is a wedding, an illness or a death. The presence of animals means that flies are inevitable—on the manure in the pens, in the kitchen, on the baby. The second factor that increases a child's vulnerability is undernutrition. In Sagada, young babies usually seem quite sturdy. Their diet of breastmilk is generally supplemented by rice water and sweetened tea. Nutrition is more of a problem for the village's older youngsters. Lee compared the local health records of fifty-nine Sagada children, twenty-five months old or younger, with the weight norms for Filipino children of equivalent ages. She found that 61 percent of the Igorot youngsters—thirty-six children—appeared to be malnourished, according to the internationally used but often debated Harvard scale of weight norms. Thirty-seven percent suffered from first-degree malnutrition and 24 percent from the more serious second-degree malnutrition. Significantly, of the 36 children only six were under a year old, so it was mostly children aged one to two who were no longer getting sufficient food to maintain normal growth. Some of the village women pointed out to Lee how thin children were after they stopped breastfeeding. The data support a correlation between termination of breastfeeding and the onset of malnutrition (Puffer and Serrano 1976, Puffer 1979). Though they will hopefully not die of malnutrition, these undernourished youngsters are far more susceptible to infection. A cold can turn into pneumonia, a case of mild diarrhea can become so severe that within 24 hours the child is dehydrated and in peril.

The health of the children of Sagada depends on having both breastmilk *and* additional suitable foods available. An unsuitable supplement may become dangerous for the weaning, as with non-fat dry milk. On the other hand, even a small amount of breastmilk is nutritionally beneficial. Camote, a starchy food, contains incomplete proteins, so-called because they can only be used by the body when combined with other proteins, such as those in breastmilk. Thus, because a little milk increases the nutritional value of the camote, where additional food is scarce, the longer a mother breastfeeds the better.

It is important, however, not to imbue breastmilk with magical substances. In fact, except in the first few months of life, for most women it does *not* meet a baby's nutritional needs. That's why supplementary foods are equally important to consider.

As I mentioned in the previous chapter, at the time we started the breastfeeding study too many medical authorities in the West were convinced that mother's milk was all a baby needed for the first 12 months of life. However, our field reports—not only from Sagada but also from the other communities we studied—revealed that mothers give their babies other foods in addition to breastmilk from a very early age.

At first we were baffled. However, within the last few years, more of the mystery has been uncovered. In Cambridge, England, researchers studying the volume of milk most lactating mothers produce in The Gambia and in England report that mother's milk production increases for the first three months after birth, then "thresholds," (as these researchers called it, that is, levels off) and tends to slowly decrease after a few more months (Whitehead et al. 1980). Thus, infants must have other foods if they are to continue growing; the amount of breastmilk available no longer increases with the child's need. Of course, some mothers do not have an adequate supply even up to three months while others can nurse exclusively for some months more. That means that in Sagada among families who can't afford much in the way of supplementary foods, some youngsters are already poorly nourished and stop growing by four or five months though they are breastfeeding very well.

The overriding issue everywhere is the additional food. Can families afford other foods for their children? Is it sufficient for the child to maintain normal growth? Is the additional food all starch or does it have some protein? Though powdered and tinned milk are sold in the small village stores, how many families can actually afford them?

To make matters worse, Igorot youngsters refuse to eat green vegetables, a common response of young children around the world. Parents are very indulgent with their children and don't force them to eat what they don't like. Somehow, though, these women lovingly cajole and trick their youngsters into eating so that most of them survive and grow up.

During her summer in Sagada in 1976, Lee renewed friendships with many of the women she had known years earlier. Among them was Agnep, whose lifestyle was very different from Odani's. At 29, Agnep had a college degree, was married to a government surveyor, and taught in the local high school. (Remarkably, most of the students who complete high school in Sagada—and better than half of them do—manage to go on to college.)

Agnep and her husband had three children, the oldest just four years old. However, there were eight in their household, since her mother lived with them and they had two high school boys as boarders. They all lived in one of the shiny, wooden framed houses covered with galvanized iron sheets that lined the main road running through the village. The house had three small rooms and a kitchen shed out back, so that the smoke from the wood fire was kept out of the house.

The furnishings were quite simple: a few hand-made pine tables and chairs, sleeping mats that were rolled up out of the way during the day, wood boxes like small foot lockers to hold clothing. Agnep, like any proper Sagada housewife, saw that the wooden floors were swept many times a day and polished every week. Visitors removed their shoes at the front door. It was drafty and not as aesthetic as the picturesque thatched-roofed cottage in the *ili* but there were far fewer rats.

Agnep came from a poor family, and the few rice-growing fields she had inherited were now rented out because there was no one to work them. She and her husband both had jobs, and her mother was too old for the hard work in the fields. Besides, Agnep needed her to take care of the children while she taught. Since the family grew no rice, they had to buy what they needed and with inflation that was increasingly a disadvantage.

When Lee stopped in after school one day to see Agnep, they sat and talked in a large, empty classroom; it had the familiar blackboard and rows of desks. Agnep, who was small and slender, usually wore Western clothes: a simple cotton shirt-waist dress or a skirt and blouse, made by a local seamstress. Though she was shy and soft-spoken, she became very ani-mated as she talked to Lee. She had put herself through col-lege with some help from a government scholarship, working first as a live-in housekeeper, then as manager of the college canteen.

A year after graduating Agnep married, and a year later her first child was born in a large city hospital. Her husband wasn't allowed to stay with her during her labor or delivery, and she recalled that she felt frightened and alone. Generally, urban hospitals in the Philippines exclude the husband. For that reason, most women from Sagada prefer to deliver in the local hospital if they don't have the baby at home.

Agnep stayed in the hospital for five days, and for the first three, the hospital staff wouldn't let her put her child to breast. The nurses insisted that colostrum (which is produced by the breasts before the "true" milk comes in) was bad for the baby. Because newborns are kept in a separate nursery, Agnep had to comply with this regulation. (In the rural hospital in Sa-gada, the older, more conservative doctors tell mothers not to breastfeed for the first 24 hours. However, the mothers have their babies with them, and one woman told Lee that she sim-ply waited until the nurse turned her back, then put the baby to her breast.)

Actually, since colostrum contains substances that are pro-tective against some bacteria, early nursing could have bene-fitted Agnep's child. She too might have been helped, since the stimulation from the suckling babe causes the uterus to con-tract and quickens the reversion to normal size. However, the "true" milk comes in around the third day whether or not the baby nurses. In many cultures colostrum is tabooed, but in some, women are expected to nurse the newborn from birth on. (Opinions on the "early milk" of cows differ in European cultures. In France a special cheese is made from colostrum, while in other countries where people believe it is dangerous for the baby, it is thrown away.)

As soon as Agnep got home from the hospital, her mother

came to stay with her, and, according to custom, she and Agnep's husband took over all household chores. For a month Agnep wasn't allowed to lift anything heavier than a chair. She was warned against activities considered too strenuous for a *mensakot*. She smiled as she recalled how her mother lovingly bathed and massaged her with warm herbal water. That period of her life was *naganas*, she said—very enjoyable.

Agnep returned to her teaching job two months after the birth of each child. While she was at work, her mother or her mother-in-law—whoever was then in charge—gave the baby one or two bottle-feedings a day of evaporated milk, diluted with boiled water and sweetened. Agnep came home at lunch to breast-feed. Most other business and professional women (the village has women doctors, nurses, midwives and storekeepers) had a more convenient routine. The baby's caretaker would bring the child to them where they worked so that they could breast-feed.

Agnep's third child refused the bottle, which caused her considerable anxiety. She said that at first the baby cried a lot while she was away, but eventually he adjusted to a pattern of fewer feedings during daytime and more frequent breast-feeding at night. Once her babies were about four months old, Agnep dispensed with bottles and began giving them rice porridge. Now she offered evaporated milk only occasionally, and from a cup.

At the time of Lee's fieldwork, Agnep's youngest child was six months old and his feeding regimen was well established. Agnep breastfed him as soon as she got up at 5:30 in the morning and again before she left for work at 7:30 A.M. At about 11:00 she came home for lunch. She fed the baby then, and again at 4:00 P.M. when she came home for the day. She also slept with him and breastfed "many times" during the evening and the night.

The combination of teaching and looking after a family was tiring and sometimes very discouraging. Agnep's mother spent the day carrying the baby around in the blanket sling, so when Agnep returned in the afternoon she had all the household chores to do herself. The boys who boarded with her were helpful and always fetched the firewood, but they, too, were gone for much of the day. There are virtually no modern conveniences in Sagada. Agnep did her laundry by hand in cold water—water, that during the five-month dry spell, had to be fetched from a community tap some distance away. She cooked over a wood stove, threshed her own rice, raised pigs and chickens, and had to feed and care for them all. In addition, when relatives or neighbors were sick, she was expected to help out—all this, plus grading school papers and preparing the next day's work.

She, at least, had her mother. Other women Lee talked with said their biggest problem was finding reliable help to look after the children. One woman complained that she often had to take on caretakers whose abilities she didn't trust; they were the only people available. The young women who might have been babysitters preferred to move to the city to work in department stores and restaurants.

When her first child was 8 months old, Agnep stopped breastfeeding because the baby was "eating well." As is the Igorot custom, once the mother made up her mind, she simply stopped—suddenly and completely. Inevitably, this was traumatic for the baby, who had always been allowed to have the breast whenever she wanted, and often painful for the mother as well, because her breasts became engorged with milk. However, the Igorot have a custom that mitigates the trauma for the toddler: Agnep used her mother—who wasn't living with her at that time—as a "weaning doula." She chose a day when the grandmother could take the child home with her and from that moment on breastfeeding was over. The baby slept with her grandmother for three days. She was fed rice porridge during the day, and when she fussed at night she was given cookies that had been dipped in sugared tea to soften them. On the fourth day the child returned home. She continued to share her mother's bed until the birth of the next baby, lessening the shock of the sudden separation. Sometimes in Sagada, when a grandmother isn't available to serve as the weaning doula, the father will distract the baby by tying her on his back during the day and sleeping with her, apart from the mother, at night.

With breastfeeding no longer part of her life, Agnep increased her baby's helpings of rice porridge and sugared tea, adding an occasional cup of warm, sugared milk or cocoa. When the child was about a year old, she began to eat what the rest of the family ate: rice, moistened with water from the vegetable pot, and camote. She was offered leafy vegetables and squash, but since she didn't like them, she wasn't forced to eat them.

Agnep's family, though far better off than Odani's, also lived chiefly on a diet of rice and camote, though they ate other vegetables and fruits. The older children occasionally had condensed milk. Lee observed that the main difference in eating patterns between the poor and the more well-off in Sagada was the total amount of food consumed, rather than the *kind* of food.

Each of Agnep's children had been admitted to the hospital two or three times a year for a cough, sore throat, or fever, and the youngest had been hospitalized five times in the six short months since he was born. He occasionally suffered from diarrhea and Agnep was puzzled about that, since at that time the child's entire diet consisted of breastmilk and rice porridge. But childhood diarrhea is not uncommon in this community where there is no running water or refrigeration.

One of the older women, who gave Lee many insights about the culture, credited the hospital for the fact that most Igorot children today live to be adults. "In the old days," she said, "if a mother had eight children, two or three would survive. That is why we do not speak of the old taboos so much to our children (i.e., tell them what to do); because we observed all of these things, and yet it is we who lost our children."

All the same, many of the more educated women in Sagada are in conflict over some of the cultural taboos. One day, when half a dozen teachers were discussing these issues, one of them gave an example of the kind of quandary they were in: "A teacher here just lost a small baby," she said. 'When that occurred, they killed an animal and invited us all to eat. And some of us were wondering, really, why did they have to do that?"

Igorot tradition demanded that the spirits be placated after a death by a sacrifice and a sharing of meat or else they might punish the community with a run of disasters. Anyone who failed to perform the sacrifice might be held responsible for whatever went wrong afterward. Bringing food and eating extra portions is a common response to death throughout the world.

"We are at that stage in our growth where we question," one of the teachers said. "We want to change . . . but we are held back by a certain—a certain . . . ," all the other women chimed in chorus, "Fear!" For a fleeting moment Lee, who was so engrossed in this culture, also felt panicky, a very human fear of defying tradition.

These mothers were caught in the transition between the old and the new cultural values and beliefs. Lee reckoned that the old beliefs persisted partly because the people feel that the life of a young child is still precarious. Even with the new medical techniques, they did not feel they had enough control over a hostile environment. As one mother put it, "You feel afraid for your child until he can walk as well as you can."

Lee also noticed that the children of the professional women were often no healthier than children in the *ili* because, while their mothers worked, they were cared for by grandparents or servants who clung to the old ideas about what a child should eat. There was a wide range of income and education in the community among the young adults, but the parents of the more educated women came from the same social environment and lived a similar lifestyle as the parents of the poor. Every family in Sagada still had close ties to traditional, nonliterate kinsfolk and neighbors. And fortunate it was, since most women nursed their babies, and, thanks to those ties, they had the kind of support system that makes breastfeeding possible. Sagada remained a relatively stable and cohesive community in 1976.

Lee said that during her initial ten-year stay in Sagada the Igorot women taught her much of what she knows about mothering. "I consider I was really in late adolescence when I arrived in the Philippines," she said. "Even though I was 23, I was still in my formative years and these women brought me up."

"The most important lesson I learned was to accept the child's level of performance," she explained. Igorot mothers expect their children to help out in very mature ways from the time they're three or four years old. The parents encourage them with a kind of gentle but firm confrontation: Children are urged to do more and more challenging tasks and they are praised for whatever they're able to do—even if their efforts make more work for adults in the end, like the toddler who accompanies her mother to the rice fields and pulls up seedlings with the weeds. Gradually, children begin to make major contributions to the family.

"In retrospect, the fieldwork I did in 1976 was an incredible workload," she said. "It was a very intense two months but I've never been sorry I did it. I feel very close to the people and the place."

Until now, breastfeeding and other traditional patterns of child care in Sagada have resisted change. Some women, like Agnep, now use a bottle at times instead of a spoon or their fingers to feed a baby, and they use tinned milk in lieu of sugared tea and rice water, but the rhythm and patterns of care are still the same.

Lee returned to the Philippines in 1978 for two years, and, though she did not live in Sagada, she visited the village and kept her ties with her old friends. "There's a new and worrying tension in Sagada these days," she says. "People no longer feel that their mountain land and life ways are secure." The government has begun to appropriate the land and natural resources of minority groups. Though the Igorot have established their right to ownership of the land through generations of continuous use, they have no "legal" title and so are vulnerable to expropriation. People are becoming aware of this and, as the villagers become politicized and self-interest creeps in, neighbor is turning against neighbor.

As the Igorot find it harder and harder to support and educate their families by tending their rice fields, many more will leave the village and families will split up. The close-knit fabric of Igorot society may gradually unravel. For individual women like Odani and Agnep there are bound to be both advantages and disadvantages as they are drawn further into the mainstream of modern life.

Inevitably, major changes in the community will affect breastfeeding. Just how and why will become clearer as we consider other cultures in the next few chapters that have already gone through similar stages of modernization.

3

INDIA

In Melwal, the village in rural India where anthropologist Rajalakshmi Misra did her fieldwork, virtually all mothers breastfeed until the baby is at least a year old. All the same, that is still sooner than previous generations. Raji (her American nickname) Misra wrote:

Nowadays the descendants of mothers who breastfed their children till the kids were three years old, breastfeed their own babies for less than half that period . . . . The women say that they do not have enough to eat and so they get irritated if the child beyond one year or a year and a quarter comes and pesters them for breastmilk . . . . The older women do not approve and accuse their daughters-in-law of trying to copy the "city people"—to preserve their health and body and roam about in cities and towns as they wish with their husbands.

City living and modern values are serious issues in village India because every year more people migrate to urban centers from the countryside. Nearly 80 percent of India's people still live in villages and over 60 percent of them till the land, but as the nation struggles to industrialize, millions are attracted to the cities where there are better opportunities for jobs, schooling, and health care. However, the more urbanized way of life also brings with it new stresses that inevitably affect the family and the way children are raised.

Melwal is a village on the outskirts of Mysore just nine miles away—a long walk for most; a short bus ride for some. It is close enough though so that the villagers are influenced by many of the city's new patterns, especially those affecting infant health. Thus, they too have shortened the period of time before weaning is completed. Raji was acutely sensitive to these changes for she had spent many months studying another community in an isolated village in the hills, where patterns of breastfeeding had hardly changed. We'll compare them later.

Usually, urbanization and a shortened period of breastfeeding occur concurrently. But not always. There are no simple explanations for change. Despite the angry criticisms the older village women level at the "selfish mothers who follow big-city ways," few mothers in Melwal, or anywhere else, put their own pleasure before the health of their babies. So why do they nurse for a shorter number of months? Some of the reasons become clear when we look into the day-to-day life of a young mother in Melwal.

Melwal's mud-brick houses are surrounded by green fields planted with rice and millet; here and there the millet has been collected into cone-shaped haystacks. Within walking distance of the village a few half-built factories loom up in the midst of the fields just off the road. On these construction sites women work beside the men, their bright-colored sarees pulled up between their legs and tucked in at the waist to form loose pantaloons. The men stack the bricks, fill the baskets with dirt, and lift them onto the heads of the women who carry them with a statuesque bearing up the ladders.

Sujata lives in Melwal. She is a slender young woman with delicate features, luminous dark eyes, and a highly expressive face. She was 18 when Raji met her and already the mother of an 8-month-old baby named Jhoti.

At 16, Sujata had married her uncle, a young man just five years older than she was. He was her mother's younger brother. In some Hindu families marriages between uncle and niece are preferred, since this arrangement keeps the bride's dowry within the family. There are other advantages as well. India is a culture where a new bride's relationship with her mother-

in-law is often as important as the relationship with her husband, since after marriage she moves into his parents' home,
and it is his mother who has authority over her. The daughter-in-law, usually an outsider, is traditionally low in the family pecking order. It is a great relief for a young girl when her
aththai (mother-in-law) is her familiar *ajji* (grandmother) whom
she will even continue to address as *Amma*, grandmother. From
a mother-in-law's point of view, a suitable bride for her son
could hardly be better than her own granddaughter, who will
generally be obedient and lovingly care for her grandparents
in their old age. In this case, Sujata and her *ajji*—a tiny, wiry,
white-haired woman with a sunny smile—were very close.

In India most marriages are still arranged by the parents,
as Sujata's was. Just a generation ago girls were usually married before puberty, though the marriage wasn't consum-
mated until after their first menstruation. Until then the girl
continued to live with her parents. Today, brides are older than
they used to be. In south India most higher caste girls don't
marry until they are between 18 and 20; those from lower and
middle-caste families (Sujata belongs to this group) marry at
15 or 16. As soon as they reach puberty, their families begin
to think seriously about finding them a husband.

Once the parents of a boy or girl have decided on a suitable
match, a go-between approaches the other family. Nowadays,
if the young people don't already know one another, they are
introduced so that they'll have a chance to get acquainted—
usually no more than a few "dates" in public places. Afterwards, if they have no serious objections, the engagement is
announced.

Weddings are grand occasions in south India, and festivities
can go on for days depending on the family's resources. This
is the family's major expense. Parents save for years often going
into debt, to provide lavish gifts for the young couple and to
put on as grand a showing as possible. Often, the status of the
bride's family hangs in the balance. If the wedding is less than
what the community expects, it can make it harder for them
to arrange for suitable marriage partners for their other children.

Raji wrote that today, even in Mopala deep in the countryside, lavish weddings have become the norm. "Previously in Mopala there used to be marriage by elopement or sometimes by kidnapping," she said. "These were the two popular forms. Now, even there the marriage is by arrangement. They like the pomp and show of the marriage, though they're very poor and it drags them into more economic crisis. But they think, 'Now I have achieved a status in the society.' "

After her elaborate wedding, Sujata moved to Melwal to live in Ajji's home—she'd grown up in a village ten miles away. The mud brick house roofed with tiles had a big central room, about 30 feet by 20 feet, called the *thotti*. It functioned as a courtyard as well since the middle portion was a sunken area several steps lower than the rest of the room, and the roof, which was supported by pillars, did not extend over this central space. Consequently, there was a great deal of light and air. During the monsoon season rain poured into the courtyard but the sunken area below was well drained so the rest of the *thotti* and all the small rooms that opened off it remained dry.

The family shared the *thotti* with eight cows, their calves, and a flock of chickens. The cows were tethered on one side of the room on the upper level, and the rafters above them were stuffed with hay. The *thotti* usually smelled fresh, partly because of the open courtyard and partly because it was swept clean several times a day.

The family consisted of Sujata and her husband, Ashoka; his parents (her grandparents); his three brothers and their wives and children. Extended families like this one live in the same house and pool their resources, at least as long as the parents are alive. Each married unit has a tiny bedroom off the *thotti*. The sons work the land and share the food they produce or the money or grains they get in exchange for their labor. But as subsistence agriculture is replaced by a cash economy, many families, including Sujata's, are now choosing to divide up their land and other resources much earlier than previous generations did.

"The old economic system was different," said Raji.

Now it is a sort of mixed economy: Some in the family go for jobs and some work on the land, so there is a clash of ideas. One fellow thinks,

"Why should I slave in the sun in a hot field while my brother sits in an office?" Or maybe one brother gets more income because besides his share of the land he has a job outside, so he thinks, "Why should I share my income?" As long as it is a common family, they have one hearth and the food they have is cooked for all together. But once the property is split it means they all provide for themselves separately and everything becomes different. Nobody wants to share the responsibilities then.

The brothers and parents of Sujata's husband live in the same house but each family keeps its share of the income and cooks separately as well. The young couples seem to prefer this arrangement, though it creates more work for the women. Raji suggests that this separate and independent living pattern can undermine the close family feeling that once existed. Those who prefer the new lifestyle say that it leads to less conflict and more privacy. At any rate, in Sujata's family, because she is granddaughter as well as daughter-in-law, the old couple chose to share her hearth. Surely they had that in mind when they were considering marriage partners for their son.

For a while after her marriage, Sujata helped Ajji in the house and in the fields as she had previously helped her mother. It was easier for her to make the adjustment to this new village since many of the inhabitants were her relatives. Melwal's population of 2,000 included members of 17 different castes. Sujata is a Vokkaliga, a group near the Vaisya caste— below the Brahmins, who are at the apex of the Hindu social structure, yet far above the untouchables, who were renamed Harijans (the children of God) by Mahatma Gandhi.

Caste obligations and proscriptions permeate Sujata's life. They determine what she is allowed to eat, how the food is cooked and served, what she wears, the construction and furnishing of her home, her age at marriage, the way her marriage is celebrated, who her friends are, and many of the basic assumptions that govern her life, such as her value of herself as a wife and a mother.

India's caste system is a series of cultures-within-a-culture. Though change is occurring more and more rapidly in the village, new behaviors tend to be incorporated into the caste system rather than change it. People inherit their caste, along with their occupation. Raji pointed out that less than 1 percent of all Hindu marriages are outside of one's birth caste.

Because the caste system includes complex ideas about the power of one group to "pollute" another, members of many castes do not eat with people who belong to other castes, nor do they accept food prepared by them. When someone breaks these rules, purifying rituals are performed. "The rules are maintained more by the women than by the men," Raji said, "because women have the opportunity. The men go to the city almost daily now that there are local buses. On the bus or in a tea shop in the city, they do not know who is sitting next to them. The women, mostly still at home, can afford to practice these food segregation customs, and the men take pride that their women are maintaining these rules." But Raji admits, those women who firmly maintain these codes and avoid contact with people in other castes also exclude themselves from many activities outside the home.

As a new bride, Sujata was permitted to leave her husband's home and return to her mother's house during the first year of her marriage for the period of time called Ashada (during June and July). She missed her mother and friends, and joyfully went home for this short period. Tradition requires that the young couple be separated during Ashada so they won't have intercourse during that month. Most of the women of Melwal couldn't say why it was important for couples to abstain during Ashada. Raji recalled, "I asked different people in different castes if they could explain. Most just said traditionally they have been avoiding that month, but the Brahmins told me if a child is conceived during Ashada and then is born on a particular day nine months later, under a particular star, that could bring disaster down upon the father." So to protect the young man, they send the wife away.

It's usually only during the first year of marriage that a wife goes home to her mother during Ashada. However, it seems likely that during this extremely warm season, couples voluntarily abstain, for the statistics show more babies are born during the rainy season (nine months after the end of Ashada) than at other times of the year. The women say that

that's good, since the weather is cooler then and the mother can rest more comfortably.

Sujata became pregnant eight months after her marriage. Probably no one ever talked to her about pregnancy or sex, because in most Indian families such subjects are never discussed. "Even today we don't talk to our sisters or children about sex or childbearing," Raji said. "They know only what they've seen, or heard at school or from their friends."

Throughout her pregnancy, Sujata carried on with her work as usual. She did not see a doctor at all; pregnant women consult them only if something seems to be wrong. From the time it was apparent she was pregnant, relatives and friends of the family began to stop by bringing gifts of food. In India the first pregnancy is a very special event—a cause for celebration. Raji explained, "Whenever people cook something good, they say, 'There is a pregnant woman in that house, we must give her a little of this,' and so they give it. Ordinarily each family thinks, 'Once during that pregnancy we'll give.' But, of course, when they bring the food the girl can't eat it all herself; she must share it with others in the family. She gets enough just to sample but in her name the whole family get something." This sharing of food acknowledges, as does a wedding, the status of the family; the higher the status the more people who bring food.

Sujata's pregnancy was uneventful. She was lucky, for Raji reported that especially with the first baby miscarriages are common in Melwal. Of the 32 mothers with whom she worked, only seven had *not* had either a miscarriage or a stillbirth. Poor nutrition, often from babyhood, is a major cause. Generally, village women weigh only a little over 100 pounds when nine months pregnant. (The average 5'2" nonpregnant American woman weighs 124 pounds.) Poor women labor in the fields or on construction sites up to the time the baby is born.

When Sujata's time was near, she went to her mother's house as is the custom in south India. She stayed there without her husband until the baby was born and for about four months afterward. Most young women welcome the chance to go home for childbirth, where their mother and sisters will care for them, grudging them nothing, and they are free from the strain and the formal behavior required of a daughter-in-law in her husband's home.

Sujata was fortunate to be able to go home. There is a tendency nationwide for this custom to break down, Raji reported, especially among those who move from the countryside into the city. Frequently, a young couple can't afford to send the wife home to her mother's village for childbirth, nor can they afford to have her mother come to them for the critical perinatal period. Feeding an extra member of the household has always been a hardship for the poor, but adding the cost of travel often makes this visit impossible. In addition, there must be someone available who can take over the mother's work at home so she can be free to care for her daughter and grandchild. If, as we've explained, the traditional support system is not present breastfeeding often fails to get off to a good start, the milk supply is affected and the infant is in danger.

Sujata's baby was born at the village clinic. She and her mother decided against having the birth at home with a midwife from the clinic, though many young women still prefer that. The baby was a girl, always a disappointment, at least for the first child in rural cultures where boys are essential. As the old women explain it, daughters soon marry and move away, while sons remain at home to support their parents in their old age. (Raji was once told by a mother whose two-year-old son had recently died, while his twin sister survived, "We take such good care of the boys," the woman said ruefully, "and then it's the girls who live.")

The cultural preference for boys doesn't mean that daughters aren't cherished. Sujata's baby was healthy, alert, very responsive and adored by all.

Like most young mothers in India, Sujata didn't try to breastfeed until her milk came in on the third day after birth. Meanwhile, a nurse gave the baby sugar water with a bottle. Because Jhoti was born in a clinic, her young mother did not adhere to all the traditional practices. For example, she didn't dose Jhoti with castor oil to help expel the "dirt" in her intestines—a long-accepted custom. Traditionally, the mother "oils" the gut three times a day until her milk comes in. Her hand-motions are patterned and graceful; she dips her right index finger in the oil, rocks it in the palm of her left hand to warm it, then rolls it onto the baby's tongue.

It's also the custom to "waste" the first milk from a woman's breasts, since many people believe it's bound to be bitter and indigestible. If the new mother's mother is in attendance, she helps her expel the milk by pressing behind the nipple with a cloth; this is done three or four times at intervals of about an hour and a half before the mother finally puts the baby to her breast.

Sujata stayed at the health center for five days; in developing countries the usual postpartum stay in a medical facility is much shorter. When she returned to her mother's house, she was put to bed in a room off the *thotti* with the door closed. Her mother and other older women kept her company and attended to her needs. "After childbirth, families don't like to expose the new mother to the air," Raji explained.

For the first 10 or 15 days after Jhoti was born (a period called *banathanam* in Kannada, the language of the region), the variety of foods offered Sujata was quite limited since so many foods are considered bad for a woman just starting to breastfeed. She was warned that if she ate jackfruit (a large fruit with edible seeds) the baby might have convulsions. She was cautioned to avoid bananas, eggs, eggplant, tomatoes, pumpkin, and potatoes, and for the most part she did.

On the other hand, she was urged to eat certain other foods to increase her milk supply. Rice with pepper water was a favorite. Raji explained that pepper water is a general term for the soup of the poor: For new mothers it was made from tamarind juice boiled with spices and lots of garlic, since garlic is thought to improve the flow of breastmilk. Whenever the family can afford it, the mother is given milk and *ghee*—butter that has been boiled. Raji recalled, "When my own son was born my mother gave me pepper water with rice as well as *ghee* and certain vegetables." Beans, carrots, okra, and *subjgai* (a kind of fennel) are also thought to be lactogenic (to increase the supply of breastmilk). So are coconut and spices.

If all is well, a new mother has two meals a day, one around eleven in the morning and the other at seven in the evening.

Today some households also provide a breakfast of bread or *uppitu* (cream of wheat cooked with oil, spices, and, when possible, vegetables) and coffee.

In those first weeks after Jhoti's birth, Sujata was thoroughly pampered and given lots of emotional support. Like new mothers in Sagada, she had an oil massage every three or four days, followed by an extremely hot bath. After that, she retied a length of fabric tightly around her waist "to prevent" (lessen) *vayu*, abdominal cramps. On massage days she was also served a little bit of mutton or chicken with her pepper water and rice.

As a new mother, Sujata was not supposed to come into contact with cold water for several months. She was not to drink it or wash with it. Her mother—her doula—and the other women of the household heated water for her, cooked for her, and scrubbed her laundry.

The prohibition against cold water is taken very seriously in south India, but people do make adjustments. One woman in Melwal had no family to care for her after childbirth, so her husband stayed home with her. After 15 days he had to go back to work, so whenever she had to touch cold water she peeled and partially mashed two pods of garlic, wrapped them in thin fabric, and plugged her ears with them. She hoped that by taking these precautions, she could preserve her health and her breastmilk.

Sujata stayed in her mother's house for four months. In the fifth month (tradition says it must be an odd-numbered month), the family consulted an astrologer, who picked an auspicious day for her to return to Melwal. On that day her husband came to pick her up. Once home, her life soon assumed a predictable pattern. One day Raji asked her to describe in detail what her day was like. By that time Jhoti was 8 months old.

"Each morning the baby wakes me around 6:00 A.M.," Sujata said. "She sleeps with me and Ashoka, so I just prop myself up to breastfeed." Like most Indian mothers, she breastfed whenever Jhoti seemed hungry, though by now the baby had settled down to a more regular routine.

"Once Jhoti is done, I put her on the floor in the *thotti* while I sweep the room," she reported. As she sweeps, other members of the household bustle about, getting organized for their own working day. "Next I have to wash the cooking vessels left from dinner the night before. At night by lamplight it's hard to tell whether a pot has been scrubbed clean, so I leave them to do in the morning." Sujata always fetches the water the night before, filling a copper jug again and again at the tap outside on the street. She balances the jug on top of her head and carries it home to pour into a tub in the *thotti*.

Once the pots are clean, she makes breakfast. Raji described her stove, which is in a room off the *thotti*, as a long box, made of mud that has been baked hard. Sujata pokes wood and kindling into it through a hole at the bottom. The top has three round openings for the cooking pots. On many mornings breakfast is fried rice, and Sujata always cooks for four: for herself, Ashoka, and his parents.

Between 8:00 and 8:30 A.M. the house gradually empties out. Ashoka sets off on his bicycle for the chipboard factory where he works as a clerk, taking along a lunch of fried rice. Sujata's grandparents (also parents-in-law) head for the fields outside the village to work their land, and other members of the household leave for jobs or their fields, while the children run off to the village school.

Even the family cows are gone, shambling along the packed dirt streets of the village toward the fields. They will graze and when needed will be tethered to pull a plough or a cart. As Sujata's *ajji* explained it, though "foreign cows" might be good only for milking, Indian cows produce milk and do the work of oxen as well. (Raji observed dryly, "Like Indian women, Indian cows are exploited.")

As the house grows quiet, Jhoti settles down for her morning nap while Sujata does the laundry. She soaks her sarees and other clothing in the tub, spreads them out on the concrete floor in the sunken center of the courtyard, and scrubs them with a bar of soap. Then she takes each garment and slaps it again and again against the floor, pounding out the soap and dirt. Once the clothes are rinsed, they are hung to dry on lines strung between the wooden posts that support the roof.

Every third day Sujata takes a bath. Her house has neither

running water nor an outhouse (which would be considered disgusting); like almost everyone else in Melwal, she and her family use the fields as a latrine. There is also no bathtub (Indians believe sitting in one's own bath water is dirty), so Sujata follows the traditional practice: She heats water on the mud stove and then, squatting near a drain in the *thotti*, washes her hair and body while pouring the warm water over herself with a cup.

"At around 10 o'clock Jhoti wakes up hungry and I feed her with Farex," she told Raji. "It's already cooked and I make it into a paste by adding cow's milk and sugar." Farex is a widely advertised modern weaning food, a blend of wheat, maize, and rice fortified with vitamins and minerals; some mothers mix it with pepper water instead of milk if the baby seems to prefer that.

Sujata feeds Jhoti on her lap, using her fingers to tuck gobbets of food into the baby's mouth. In India there's a special etiquette for eating—only with the right hand and the first two joints of the fingers. Sujata fed Jhoti without a wasted motion, deftly popping the food in and wiping the extra bits off the baby's face, her fingers becoming first a spoon and then a napkin, neatly alternating with a rhythm, smooth and sure.

When Jhoti became restless and began to refuse the food, Sujata stood up, balanced the baby on her hip, and began to walk about, distracting Jhoti as she slipped more of the Farex into her mouth. She carried the bowl of porridge in her left hand and fed the baby with her right. Raji explained that walking the baby during a feeding is a common practice in India. "Parents like to make the baby sit and feed but after a certain stage the baby refuses to sit in one place like a gentleman. The mother's intention is somehow to stuff into him whatever portion of food she has taken for him, so she walks around to distract his attention."

Sujata's family could afford to buy Farex. She began using it when Jhoti was six months old, the usual age in Melwal for introducing a baby to semi-solid food. However, most village mothers still use a gruel made from ragi millet. They must go through a tiresome routine to prepare it that begins with soaking the grain overnight and tying it in a cloth until it sprouts. Then they dry it, fry and grind it, sieve it through thin fabric, and store the powder they've produced in a tightly closed tin. The mother will mix this powder with small amounts of water and salt and boil it to make a thick porridge. Raji noted that different villages in India favor different first foods for a baby. In other communities mothers make a similar rice or wheat gruel, or tapioca, or they dry bananas to make a powder that can be made into gruel.

"Jhoti has had other foods now too, of course," Sujata told Raji, "like *roti* (similar to Middle Eastern pita bread) and rice. When she first had rice we had a celebration, and Ajji (the baby's grandmother) was the one to give it to her." The rice was cooked until it was soft, and Ajji mashed it with *ghee* and a pinch of salt to form a paste, then put a bit of it on the baby's tongue.

Once Jhoti had her mid-morning feeding, Sujata began to prepare lunch, which might be a dish like rice with pulse curry (pulse is a small bean similar to a split pea). When Jhoti fussed, Sujata would pick her up and, balancing her on her left hip, would continue to stir the rice.

About noon, Raji said, Sujata breastfed the baby again. At 1:00 P.M. her grandparents arrived home for lunch. It's the custom for women and their grown daughters to eat after the men and children finish. So, her grandfather ate first, and afterward Sujata and Ajji had lunch together. In most households the daughter-in-law eats last, but because Ajji was Sujata's grandmother, they ate together. "The women also think men should be served more (food) because they are toiling more, whether they really are or not," Raji added. "The assumption is that the man requires more energy and his build is bigger also, so he requires more food."

After lunch the old couple returned to the fields, and Sujata and Jhoti napped for a while. Jhoti generally woke up hungry at around 3:30 P.M. and was breastfed. At 4:00 Sujata got up, washed the cooking vessels left from lunch, and then swept the house once more. At about 5:00 Ajji came home and played with and cared for the baby. Sujata's grandfather usually stayed in the fields for a while longer and was joined by Ashoka, who went directly from the factory to the fields to put in a few hours of work. The men arrived home at different times.

Around 6:00 P.M., Sujata breastfed again, then she started making dinner, which might be a rice and okra curry. In all, Sujata generally used a little over three pounds of rice a day to feed four adults. The men had dinner at about 8:00 P.M. and again, Sujata and Ajji ate later.

At 9:00 Sujata gave Jhoti cow milk. She mixed half a cup of water with half a cup of the milk and some sugar, boiled it, cooled it, then fed it to the baby with a spoon. She would have preferred to use a bottle, but bottles are expensive. About a month earlier, at the age of seven months, Jhoti had suddenly turned cranky and seemed hungry even after breastfeeding, so Sujata knew that her breastmilk was no longer sufficient for the baby's needs, even with the mid-morning feeding of Farex to supplement it. As soon as she began offering Jhoti cow milk in the evening, Jhoti settled down and once more began sleeping through the night.

In Melwal it is unusual for a family who has a cow to give its milk to a child, unless they are relatively well off. "They think mother's milk is best," Raji explained. "They say, 'Why should we give cow milk? Let us cash this milk.' So they walk all the way to Mysore city and sell it off." Since Sujata's family had two cows and they produced about three quarts a day, she was able to sell two quarts and keep one for the family. Most families are so desperate for cash they can't afford *not* to sell *all* the milk their cows produce.

Raji felt that the average diet in Melwal probably supplied enough calories but was short on protein. For most families the chief staple was ragi millet, since the price of rice had increased dramatically in recent years and it was now almost a luxury item. Though Sujata's family could afford to have rice more often than most, she also served ragi regularly, often as *hittu*, balls of dough.

"My husband (who is a professor and comes from north India) tried *hittu* once or twice," Raji recalled. "We are used to munching everything and so he tried to munch it, but it's all paste and sticks to the palate and he couldn't get it down," she laughed. "The technique is to dip it in curry, put it in the mouth, and swallow it whole."

In Melwal the upper caste villagers are vegetarian by tradition. However, the poorer families of all castes seldom have meat, since they cannot afford it. In 1982 a kilogram (2.2 pounds) of mutton cost $3, and the average family earned about $20 a month. Families had meat only during festivals. Then three or four households might pool their money to buy a goat, when an animal sacrifice was required. "It's terrible in the village now," Raji said. "They have fruit only when people are sick; then four oranges or apples will come into the family. Vegetables they take because what they grow they consume, but that is seasonal. Many vegetables are not grown in Melwal, and in these villages there is no vegetable market at all. Very rarely do people go to the city or some other distant place to buy vegetables."

Most poor families spend over 60 percent of their income on food, and both adults and children are thin, even gaunt. When Raji recorded the weights of thirty-three village women, all but one weighed under 100 pounds, while most of the men in the village weighed under 110. In the United States the average woman and man weighs 25 to 30 pounds more.

Despite deficiencies in their diet, virtually all mothers in Melwal breastfeed. In fact, out-and-out failure to breastfeed is so rare that no one could remember any case of it. However, in the process of feeding, women do find at some point that their milk is no longer sufficient, and this happens sooner to some than to others. If it occurs when the baby is still quite small, a mother will complain that she herself isn't getting enough to eat, or she would blame her own tensions or sorrows. Most of the Melwal women say the milk comes in when the baby begins to breastfeed, but they had not thought about how the ejection reflex works nor how it relates to the milk supply; nonetheless, they often acknowledge that stress interferes with breastfeeding.

When a baby cries persistently and obviously isn't getting enough to eat, most mothers at first try to increase the flow of breastmilk by eating foods considered to be lactogenic, such as pepper water. They believe cow milk is especially important for a breastfeeding woman, yet many cannot afford to drink even a small cup a day. When that doesn't help, then provided the woman can afford it, she gives cow or buffalo milk to the baby to supplement her breastmilk—as Sujata did. Families who can't provide milk introduce soft solids such as gruel earlier than they would have liked.

Women from families poorer than Sujata's often work, leaving the baby at home with their mother-in-law or with an older daughter. The family's financial status generally determines if the mother will be able to put off her return to work until the baby is at least six months old. As far as Raji could estimate, the poorer the family the sooner the mother has to return to work. Working mothers in Melwal, like those in Sagada, continue to breastfeed night and morning, and while they are away the baby is given cow milk, if possible, or gruel. Only rarely, if the baby is distraught would an accommodating relative breastfeed the child.

No infant formula was available in the village; few families had the money to buy it. The women knew about processed milk because they had sisters in Mysore who used it, but when Raji asked them to recall any brand names, they couldn't.

The young mothers of Melwal generally give up breastfeeding once the baby is taking solid foods well at a year or a year plus a few months. When the time comes, Sujata will undoubtedly take Ajji's advice on how to taper off gradually; traditionally, the mother-in-law guides a young mother with the first baby. As a rule, the change proceeds smoothly, though some mothers recalled a particular child who demanded the breast so persistently that they finally smeared their nipples with the juice of bitter leaves or fruit to discourage him.

In the past, a woman breastfed until she became pregnant, often for a good three years, and the youngest child in the family might still be given the breast at the age of five more as a comfort than for milk. In fact, many of the older women are quick to criticize when their daughters-in-law decide to give up breastfeeding after only one year. They can't understand why a mother would stop except for a pregnancy. Both young and old agree that it is dangerous to breastfeed while pregnant. Sujata's *ajji* explained that by the time the mother is three or four months pregnant, a change occurs in her milk, and if she keeps on breastfeeding after that the baby might develop diarrhea. (The women of Sagada in the Philippines also warned of this danger.) Raji noted that babies who are removed from the breast too soon, because their mothers are pregnant, are usually listless, clingy, or cry a lot, and often they become sick.

Indian mothers know that breastfeeding usually prolongs the interval between pregnancies, but they also know full well that they can't always count on it.

To prevent conception and allow the mother to continue breastfeeding until the baby is old enough to be safely weaned, couples are expected to abstain from intercourse for six months to a year after the baby's birth. Abstention is crucial, for too frequent pregnancies take a toll on many of these frail women. And, as the proverb goes, "the infant that is buried will come back to the womb immediately." Few of the village women use artificial birth control devices, despite vigorous government promotion, though many, after having several children *who live*, choose sterilization. In contrast with the older women who had ten or twelve babies—and often half of them died—the younger generation averages five or six.

"They are going for tubectomies, for tying the tubes," Raji explained. "It's usually done soon after the birth of the baby. Though many people don't like to go for this tubectomy, still they've started learning the lesson that fewer children give them greater prosperity."

The village women said that for three or four months after they stop breastfeeding, their babies seem tense and anxious. The children miss the comfort of nursing and have to get used to digesting the family food. It is a dangerous time. They don't eat properly at first and often lose weight.

In Melwal infant mortality is very high by Western standards. Undoubtedly, part of the reason is that mothers can't give their babies sufficient, safe foods in addition to breastmilk. Nevertheless, in recent years the death rate has dropped not only in this village but throughout India. Medical care has improved, and Melwal now has a primary health center, a resident doctor, and a trained midwife. A government health worker makes occasional visits to examine children and can dispense some medicines. But she isn't equipped to do regular check-ups and often doesn't even have a scale to weigh the babies.

Today in Melwal when a child falls ill the mother still tends to try traditional home-made herbal remedies first. "To put it in a crude way," Raji explained, "when the baby is unable to move its limbs, or in the case when fever persists more than two days then the mother feels she must get medical help. With diarrhea, too, they wait one or two days." Though diarrhea can be very dangerous for babies, it's hard for a mother to know which attack is critical since it is common for children to develop diarrhea as often as three times a month.

The women believe that breastmilk is the best and safest food when a baby is sick. However, a mother's milk is also sometimes blamed for what goes wrong. If a baby has diarrhea, the older women often scold the mother for eating too much ragi, saying it has affected her milk. When a breastfed baby develops a cold, they advise the mother to avoid eating certain foods that might make the child's cold worse.

Why is it that in Melwal today's young mothers stop breastfeeding sooner than their own mothers did? Part of the answer lies in the changes that have occurred in village life. The village now has its own schools; there are taps in the streets so that it's no longer necessary to walk long distances to a well; and though the unemployment rate is 40 percent, there are actually more jobs available than in the past. On the other hand, most villagers work in the fields, and in the lean periods between sowing and harvesting seasons many families have trouble making ends meet.

Population has increased, and food prices have risen so dramatically that many of the villagers are actually poorer and hungrier than ever before. Raji reported that in some homes wedding pictures show the brides of previous generations dressed in more elaborate sarees than the brides of this generation, and laden with more gold jewelry as well. Mute testimony Raji concluded, not only to declining family fortunes but also to the reduced resources of the whole village, since wedding finery is often lent to the family by other villagers.

 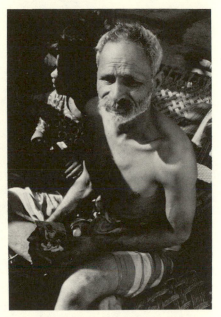

9. A father enjoys his children, 9 months and 2½ years old, in a project outside of New Delhi, December 1977.

10. December 1978: "They have gone back to God. Thank you for the pictures. We had no way to remember them."

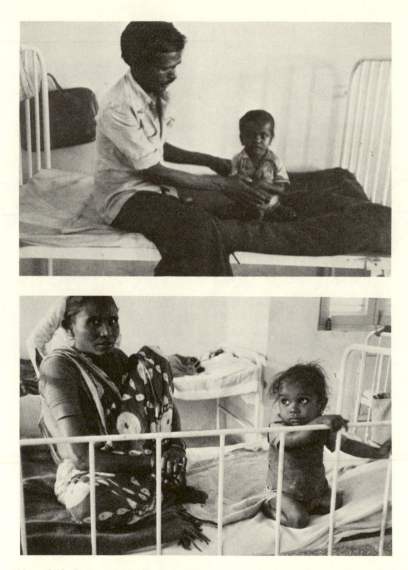

11. and 12. Parents stay with their child in the hospital, usually sharing the bed. They do most of the nursing and cook all meals.

In this village, tradition holds that a mother should stay home and tend the children, the house and the animals. Even so, women do work outside the home. In fact, today many of them must. The jobs are menial, and they admit frankly they would prefer to stay home. A young mother who goes out to work generally leaves her baby with her mother-in-law, or when that's not possible she counts herself lucky if she has a daughter, even an eight year old, to tend the younger children. Girls over 14 are considered old enough to go out to work.

Since men traditionally do no housework, when the mother returns home she faces all the usual daily tasks in addition to coping with a baby who needs to be breastfed. Traditions are changing slowly, however, and in some households where there are no other women to help out, a husband will look after the children in the evening. Raji said, "If a child keeps nagging, maybe he will shout at the child or give one a spanking. Not that he allows the woman to relax, but at least she can do the cooking so that he gets his dinner. Some men will actually feed the baby." However, there's great resistance to the change. The older generation complains that such men spoil their wives by doing too much for them, and some mothers-in-law actually seem jealous, since in their day husbands never gave such help.

Be that as it may, it's no surprise today to find a young mother, coping with work outside the home (sometimes hard physical labor) and without another woman to share the workload and baby care, ready, even eager, to give up breast-feeding as soon as it seems that the baby can manage without it.

Sujata is better off than many women in the village, but it seems likely that she, too, will stop breastfeeding once Jhoti is over a year old and taking solid foods well. She will certainly stop if she thinks the family would be better off if she worked in the fields while Ajji looks after the baby. Even if that's not the case, she's apt to stop breastfeeding at the same time as other young mothers in her village. Luckily, she can afford to give Jhoti cow milk.

Changes that are affecting the whole tenor of life in Melwal will likely have even more of an impact in the future. The city of Mysore is gradually expanding as the government promotes

industrialization around the outskirts. The area around Melwal is part of the current expansion scheme, so the government has been buying up land for factories. This means less
land is available for farming. Most villagers still worked on
the land, but the construction sites are near the village, and
men and lower caste women find jobs there. Raji predicted that
as the expansion continues, many village men will become
factory workers while the women will become servants in the
homes of wealthier women. "These people have little education," she said, "and this is what has already happened on the
other side of Mysore."

Whenever a mother has to travel a considerable distance to
a job, breastfeeding becomes more difficult. In addition, with
the change from subsistence agriculture to a cash economy, the
trend to early division of the family property will probably ac-
celerate. As families split up, with some members moving into
the city, Rajalakshmi anticipates a steady erosion of the support system that nurtures a new mother at the time breastfeeding begins.

There are villages in south India where women still breastfeed for as long as their own mothers did. Mopala village, where
Rajalakshmi Misra also conducted fieldwork, is one of them.
Up in the hillside, and far from any town or city, the more traditional customs persist. Most infants are still breastfed until
the mother becomes pregnant, usually for two, sometimes three
years. And yet the mothers in this community count themselves lucky if they can stay home for the first few months after
the birth. Because most families are very poor, the women have
to work away from the house and leave their babies home. Before they leave their bamboo-and-mud huts in the morning they
breastfeed and—keeping the baby in bed with them—they
breastfeed many times during the night.

For these village women breastfeeding is the only option. The
village stores don't carry powdered or tinned milk or infant
formula. Even cow milk is rare because there are very few cows
in the area, and most families couldn't afford it anyway. Since
it is the local custom to begin feeding babies rice gruel before
they are three months old, families use this food to tide the

baby over while the mother is at work; the mother-in-law or an older child gives the feedings.

Many other traditions are different from those practiced in Melwal. In Mopala, for instance, young couples move into their own hut as soon as they are married. And though a maternity center is located nearby, most babies are born at home. Sometimes a midwife is brought in; often the mother-in-law takes charge perhaps with one or two other women to help her. Some of the methods the women use are, as Raji put it, "undesirable." To hurry the labor along, they repeatedly dilate the cervix with their fingers. Then, after the baby is born, they wait five or ten minutes for the mother to eject the placenta and if she doesn't succeed, they again interfere.

"I have attended two childbirths in this village," Raji said, "and I have seen them take some false hair that the elderly women wear and ask the mother to swallow it. Naturally, she feels like vomiting but that's the purpose: So that when she is vomiting the placenta will be forced out." Sometimes the women would mix soot from the fireplace with hot water and give it to the mother to drink—a common practice in many areas of the world. (Currently, research is being conducted on the possible therapeutic aspects of ash.)

At one of the births Raji attended, she learned a profound lesson from the midwife in charge. "Twenty years ago," Raji said, "this woman got a fat stipend for taking a government training course in delivering babies, but I found she was doing the delivery in the traditional way. I asked her, 'How is it you have gone for this course and it doesn't seem to have any effect?' 'I went to the course for the stipend,' she admitted. 'Anyway, nobody accepts those rules for childbirth in the village, so I cannot practice them.' " New techniques often don't work when they are brought back to the village. Health professionals are now more aware that they must fit their teaching to the real world of the villager, not the other way around.

Though the people of Mopala maintain many of their traditions regarding childrearing, other areas of their lives have changed dramatically. Those of us who study these cultures often are tempted to romanticize about such pockets of ancient culture. They appear to provide the individual with a degree of security that most of us in the West have never known. Yet all traditions are not equally valuable nor do all practices change at the same rate.

"We used to share more," Mopala women say. The men would hunt together and would split the kill; building a hut was always a community effort. Today hunting is no longer possible because the forests of the region have been cleared. Most people must have a job to survive, and families now pay to have a hut built. Yet as they adjust to a cash economy, many villagers seem to prefer the trade-offs it has brought. They may have given up some of the security of close (often stifling) community ties, but they've gained a new independence.

The way a mother feeds her baby is influenced by the subsistence patterns of agricultural villages, the distance from an urban center, and the financial status of the family. This became clearer to me when I visited the Egyptian village in our project and saw how the factors converge to make a profound difference when it comes to the care and survival of infants. Let me demonstrate this by reporting a few vignettes from the lives of some Egyptian peasant mothers. Furthermore, I hope that the reader will come to agree with me after reading the story of Salwa Ahmed, a young Egyptian mother, that poverty itself is a limiting factor and that poor mothers have very little choice about how they feed their infants.

In Mit-Salama, an Egyptian village about 20 miles from Cairo, all mothers breastfeed as long as possible, usually about two years. (These women were the poorest and the most hardpressed of all those included in the HLC study.) In their village there was no sanitation system, and their diet, as with most poor agricultural peoples, was low in protein—meat was scarce. Although potable water is available in the village from public faucets, the distance to the faucet and the long line and crowding led many to use water from the Nile. The women were clearly aware they were taking a chance, but they said fatalistically, "Even water from our deepest wells sometimes hurts our bellies."

In her field notes, HLC anthropologist Soheir Sukkary recorded the story of Salwa Ahmed, a mother fairly typical of

Mit-Salama. Salwa lived in a one-room mud house. At 26, she had given birth to five children and three were still living. She breastfed all her babies but had more difficulty with her first-born. Her breasts were always sore, and when the baby was about seven months old she developed an infection. The doctor at the clinic recommended that Salwa stop breastfeeding for a while to give her nipples a chance to heal, so for three days she fed the baby sugar water. Shortly after that, the baby started vomiting and developed diarrhea. In her field notes, Soheir described what happened:

She could not wash the diapers properly because she did not have enough money for soap. The neighbors lent her money and soap on various occasions . . . . She used to take the baby to the village doctor every other day. In many cases, the doctor (was) not in the clinic, and she spent many hours waiting . . . . The baby seemed to be crying all the time, which made it very difficult for her to go to the river to wash clothing and cooking utensils.

Her breasts started to hurt because the baby was not taking his ordinary supply of milk. With the passage of time the baby was getting skinnier and very weak. A few weeks later (he) died. She said, "It was God's will," although she knows that their poverty had something to do with it.

In 1976 government records indicated that infant mortality was declining in the area around Mit-Salama. However, it was Soheir's impression from what the women told her at least in this particular village that babies were still dying as often as ever. Statistics are not reliable because many peasants fail to register the birth or death of their children, especially girl babies. The region has a hospital and a clinic, but the people avoid the hospital; their experience has given them the impression that it is a place one goes to die. The clinic doctor is often unavailable, and the medications he prescribes are too expensive or not to be found in the village dispensary.

The most dangerous period for babies is between six and ten months because by that time their mothers are producing less breastmilk yet can afford very little supplementary foods. Even from infancy they are offered bread, rice, meat broth, and sometimes fruit "to taste," but a taste is all they have. When they are about seven months old, small amounts of soft solids are gradually added to their diet. Sadly, the families find it difficult to provide even these tiny portions. Such soft foods require fuel for cooking—another costly item.

One great difference between the women of south India and those of Mit-Salama is that, no matter how poor they are, the Egyptian women cannot work outside the home. In their community a man is humiliated if his wife works for others. This will probably continue until male unemployment is reduced.

In Egypt, as in India, there has always been a strong support system for new mothers, beginning in late pregnancy. A woman traditionally returns to her mother's home about two weeks before the baby is due and remains there for about 40 days after the delivery, or if that isn't possible the young woman's mother, sister, or aunt comes to stay with her.

Today, family members who break away and leave the villages cannot always maintain these traditions. Mothers still make every effort to attend the birth of their daughter's first child because, as they say, she is still just a girl and needs her mother. However, with the second and subsequent babies, often there isn't enough stored food or extra funds for the daughter to go and stay with her mother or for her mother to come to her. Women who now live in the towns, fairly isolated from kin, find it difficult to manage a new baby and a household unless they have another child old enough to take some responsibility. If they have had a successful experience breastfeeding another child, nursing later children is much easier.

Mothers in Mit-Salama, as in India, know that if the baby is to survive they have no choice but to breastfeed. Moreover, these village women find it almost unthinkable that a woman might *not* breastfeed. They explain that breastfeeding is easier and cheaper than bottle-feeding; the milk is cleaner; babies grow bigger and are healthier; and they point out that their ancestors always breastfed. Two women said they had actually lost babies because they had to give them cow milk mixed with unclean water.

Men are particularly keen to have their wives follow the dictates of the Koran which admonishes women to breastfeed. One woman told Dr. Sukkary: "In our village all women have to breastfeed. I told my husband that I was tired of breast-feeding after seven children . . . . You know what he said? He told me even if I break my neck I still have to breastfeed."

She paused a minute to consider what she had just said, then raised her head to look straight at Soheir. "We are not city girls," she insisted proudly.

4

SARDINIA

The older women in Baru, a shepherd village in the mountains of central Sardinia, dress in black, covering their heads with a black kerchief or veil. During the growing season they spend hours almost every day working in their vegetable gardens farther up the mountain, as women in Baru have done for generations. Each summer afternoon they descend the dusty paths back to the village carrying on their heads huge tubs (now made of plastic) heaped with vegetables. Under their coarse, ankle-length heavy black skirts their abdomens are pronounced from thrusting the pelvis forward as they trudge down the mountain balancing their load.

Graziella, just one generation younger than these women, lives on the outskirts of the village in a three-story building with her husband, a college graduate, who teaches in a local school. Most people in Baru still live in two-story, stone houses with just one or two rooms on each floor. They all have a fireplace, the main source of heat for warmth and cooking. Graziella's building houses six families in modest apartments.

A small, slender but graceful woman with short black hair, she dresses most often in tailored slacks or a skirt made of blue denim material with a sweater. She has had only a fifth grade education. In 1976 she was 32 and her children were 7, 8 and 9 years old.

In some ways her lifestyle is traditional. All three of her

children were born at home with a midwife in attendance, and, as is the custom, her mother was her doula.

"How Mama encouraged me during the birth of all three!" Graziella recalled. "I wasn't afraid when she was there." Following the local tradition, her husband was present for the birth of the first child. "He saw how I suffered," she said. "He told me afterward that he cried. But for the second and third babies he didn't want to watch. He stayed in the kitchen."

For three months after her first child was born, Graziella's mother lived with her. "I didn't even get up to go to the bathroom for the first two weeks," she said. "My mother and my husband wouldn't let me get up, even if I wanted to." The period around childbirth was a particularly happy period in her life. Her mother also came to stay when the next two children were born, but she has since died; she had a heart attack one day while working in her *orto* (vegetable garden). Her daughters miss her most when they think what childbirth is like without her.

Graziella breastfed her first baby for two months. Sadly she recalled that though she drank milk and wine and ate cheese and bread—all foods older women recommend to promote a good milk supply—her son didn't grow well. When he was two months old, he weighed a few ounces less than he had at birth, and the doctor advised her to stop breastfeeding immediately and give him milk made from a powder sold at the pharmacy. "We gave him (fresh) goat milk instead," she said, "and he gained one kilo (about 2.2 pounds) a month after that."

Graziella didn't even try to breastfeed her other children. From the beginning she gave them cow milk, mixed with bottled water and offered in a bottle. When each baby was three months old, she added rice powder to the milk; at four months she gave the child a biscuit every day, and at five months, vegetable broth. By nine months they were eating table foods along with the rest of the family, including meat that was very finely cut. As the children grew older, she switched them from cow to sheep milk, which had been brought to a boil and then refrigerated.

"The greatest joy that I've had was to give birth to the first baby," Graziella said. "I felt important in that moment. It was a joy indescribable, and with every birth I felt this joy.

"I live for the family," she explained. "Everything is for the children." Yet, she added she had a yen to be more independent, to work outside the home—to teach school, have an office job, or be a midwife. "But if I worked I'd have to leave the children and I wouldn't want to leave them with another person," she said.

Mothers in many parts of the world share this reluctance to trust their young to another woman—neighbor or co-wife—sometimes fearing that someone might cast a spell over the child out of jealousy or for revenge. Or as one otherwise very modern and experimental American mother said, "I'm afraid she may not agree with the way I do things. Besides, I want her to love me the most."

What kind of life would she like her own daughter to have? "I would like her to be a medical doctor. I want her to be important!" Graziella said.

Why was she unable to breastfeed her first child? Why did she decide she wouldn't attempt to nurse the next two babies? Hundreds of medical professionals around the world are asking such questions about women like Graziella. In their world, now undergoing rapid cultural change, old values now compete with new ones, sometimes causing anxiety and distress, a state antithetical to breastfeeding.

Elizabeth Mathias, HLC's anthropologist in Sardinia, reported that in the two shepherd villages where she did her fieldwork, almost all mothers still breastfeed but they don't continue as long as their own mothers had. Those who, like Graziella, are better off financially and are moving away from the traditional village life at a faster pace, appear to stop sooner.

One older woman who had no doubt that breastfed babies are healthier, said disapprovingly to Elizabeth: "The wives of shepherds and farmers want to nurse, but the wives of teachers, lawyers, and policemen are *pavone* (peacocks). They want to be beautiful, to be admired—they feel superior—and they think breastfeeding ages them."

Is she right? Is this a case of modern attitudes intruding on traditional practices? Or is the quickening pace of cultural change responsible and inevitable?

To put these questions in perspective, let us describe the traditional life of the region and point out the significant practices that are changing.

Baru is on the main highway and is relatively prosperous compared to Seni, the other village Elizabeth studied. Baru has long had regular contact with the outside world as its young men emigrated to the continent to find jobs and returned with the money they saved and with new ideas.

Seni is more isolated, in the mountains at the end of a seemingly endless roller coaster road. There are few cars. Its beige and white stone houses spill down the hillsides, a mosaic of orange tile roofs, and the narrow cobbled stoned streets are so steep that in places they turn into steps. On all sides the mountains loom, hunched against the sky, oppressive with their bare, light grey rocks and dry bush; the air is as limpid as spring water. Most of the time only bird songs intermingle with the sounds of human voices.

In 1976 when Elizabeth was in Seni for the HLC study, most families kept a goat for milk. Every morning before dawn a young boy would come to gather the goats, driving them through the streets and up the mountains to pasture, and every evening he would bring them back. Once inside the village each animal found its own way home. In those days almost every family also kept a donkey to carry the heaviest loads; but when Elizabeth returned to Seni only four years later, in 1980, most of the donkeys were gone and motorbikes had been added.

Seni was originally settled by ten families. As a relatively isolated community of shepherds, it was self-sufficient; to a large extent it still is. Flocks of sheep, goats, and some cows supply the villagers with meat and dairy products. They grow their own vegetables. In the past they lived very humbly, barely above the subsistence level.

Seni is no longer so isolated. In 1969 the road to the village was finally paved and, just seven years later, changes already in progress in Baru were overtaking Seni as well. Most houses now had running water and flush toilets, though few had central heating, despite the fact that the temperature can drop below freezing in winter. Radios were common. Television sets were in the village bars and in a few homes, and a village about 18 miles away had a movie theatre. As in Baru in 1966, many of the young men emigrated to northern Italy or West Germany (now restricted) to find work: 200 of the village's 1,000 registered residents were living abroad at that time.

The women of Seni enjoyed discussing infant feeding with Elizabeth. They talked to her as they went about their work in the fields or in their homes, or sometimes women would stop to chat in the street; soon others would gather around. Always with notebook in hand, Elizabeth used the opportunity to get more information on feeding practices.

Elizabeth spent a great deal of time with one particular shepherd family. The grandmother, Asunta, was 64. She had had five children—four were living—and her two daughters were now women in their thirties with children of their own. Asunta had a rather gaunt face, and as is characteristic of strong, self-assured persons, she seemed taller than she was.

One day Elizabeth and I joined several family members as they were preparing for a holiday feast. A goat was slaughtered in the courtyard of the house. The atmosphere was festive and, in a mischievous mood, one of the men took the dead goat's teat and squirted milk at Elizabeth. I chortled politely, though I felt like choking. Then he cut an opening in the animal's leg and, holding it as if it were a clarinet, blew into it until the goat began to puff up. This was the traditional method of separating skin from flesh. It makes skinning the animal easier. But at the sight of the still-warm carcass being inflated like a hairy balloon, I experienced some very unscientific feelings, so I retreated to a corner of the courtyard and hid behind my camera. Not Elizabeth. She stayed right there, one shoe in a puddle of blood, watching, recording and translating the men's jokes for me.

Elizabeth frequently joined Asunta and Anna, her younger daughter, as they walked up the mountainside before sunrise to carry food to the pigs. As always, Asunta was dressed in black: skirt, blouse, shawl, stockings, and heavy work shoes.

Once the women of Seni were past middle age, it was as if they were perpetually dressed for mourning. When a relative died, they were expected to wear black for anywhere from one to several years, while a wife who lost her husband might dress in mourning for life. The matrons of the village wore bright-colored print dresses but changed to black for church, which they attended every day. Though younger women now dress in jeans, it seems unlikely that the grandmothers will ever change their garb.

Anna was a slip of a woman, barely five feet tall, with high cheekbones, delicate features, and long dark hair that she pinned up in back. She was 33 and, like most of the women her age, wore a knee-length skirt, often of blue-jeans fabric, with knee socks and heavy shoes. That evening she balanced on her head—cushioned with a thick pad of cloth—a plastic tub filled with whey for the pigs. (Whey is the watery liquid that separates from the curds in cheese-making.)

Both women had been up before sunrise. As shepherds' wives their daily routine included straining, measuring, and selling the milk produced by the family's herd of goats; making cheese; gathering wood on the common land outside the village; carrying water from the public tap in the dry season when the faucets at home went dry; feeding the pigs—a very important economic asset; doing housework and cooking; carrying lunch to their husbands miles up the mountain; and loving and scolding the children and taking them to church.

Like all the other women in the village, even the wife of the most prosperous landowner, both Anna and Asunta tend an *orto*. These gardens are in the hills above the village several miles away, just as the "swiddens" are in Sagada. The land is dry, so using long-bladed hoes they dig little channels alongside each row of plants for irrigation. To water the plants, they scoop out the mud plug at the head of each channel where it connects to the main ditch in which the water has collected. They replace the plug again when enough of the precious water has trickled down the row. When the vegetables are ripe, the women harvest them, load them into a plastic tub, and carry them on their head down the mountain. (In Seni men never carry anything on their head.) Vegetables are sometimes bartered with other families.

Anna's life had been much the same as her mother's. She worked up to the time each of her children was born, though she was careful not to do any heavy lifting. She had both babies at home—her mother and the village midwife were with her—and she began breastfeeding a short time after the birth. In other parts of Italy (and in many other cultures) mothers wait several days until the milk comes in, but not in Seni. In shepherd communities everyone knows a great deal about lactation. In fact, the men know so much from their experience with goats that women consult with them about breastfeeding. During my visit, I overheard a shepherd giving advice to a woman whose breast had become hard and engorged with milk. He recommended gentle massage and continued nursing.

In Seni, mothers frequently give an infant sugar water from a spoon on the first day or so after birth to help tide it over until sufficient "true" milk comes in. In the early weeks, they breastfeed whenever the baby cries, so the child sleeps in the mother's bed or in a cradle near her.

The new mother's support system is similar in some ways to the traditional arrangement in Sagada, in rural India and Egypt. For a while, if the new mother is not visiting at her natal home, her own mother comes to help with housework and child care while other women in the family look after her garden. The husband is not likely to do much around the house because of the distinct division of labor between men and women in Sardinia.

In Asunta's day women could rest only a few weeks after childbirth before they had to start working again in the *orto*. They generally took their babies with them, leaving them under a tree while they worked and breastfeeding them whenever they cried.

Times are better now, so the women of Anna's generation are given more time at home to adjust to their matrescence. They don't return to their fields for at least six weeks after childbirth, and when they do the baby is left at home with a relative or an older youngster for the two or three hours they work in the *orto*. Generally, they breastfeed in the morning, at lunch time, in the evening, and just before bedtime. While the mother is away, a hungry baby is fed goat or sheep milk in a bottle which might have a bit of coffee and sugar added "for flavor." From the time infants are about a month old, they are given vegetable and meat broth and cereal with a spoon. Mixed feeding—breast plus bottle plus other foods—is taken for granted in Seni.

Some women over 60 recalled a time when there was a kind of reciprocity in breastfeeding: Sisters would feed one another's babies, or an aunt and niece or mother and daughter might help one another when both had a nursing infant. This kind of sharing was kept within the family, since breastfeeding was considered an intimate, family affair. An elderly relative of Anna's once boasted to Elizabeth that one day when she was working in the fields she breastfed her own infant and nine more besides! A jolly, heavy-set woman, she attempted to convince Elizabeth that, "In my day the milk was better. The food mothers eat today is less genuine, so mother's milk isn't as nutritious."

Along with her feelings of "natural is best," she was highly suspicious of additives—the *medicinas*—in processed foods sold in the local stores. It's not uncommon for older women in many cultures to insist not only that their milk was better but also that their infants were stronger. (True, the babies who lived were strong and healthy, but how many of them died?)

The quality and quantity of breastmilk is a constant preoccupation of women. In the shepherd village in the mountains of Spain that was also a part of the HLC study, anthropologist Renate Fernandez was visiting a family one day when an old woman began lecturing her granddaughter, saying that she must "feed up" her 13-month-old baby. She was convinced that this slim young woman couldn't possibly be producing enough breastmilk to sustain the baby, even with supplements. A little later, someone fetched a cradle from the attic to show Renate. The young woman's father had slept in it when he was an infant. She placed her baby in it and his feet stuck out over the end. The grandmother was astonished. "Your father was in that cradle until he was two years old and running," she had to admit.

In Sardinia, as in other places, local lore includes beliefs and rationalizations about breastfeeding. The women say, for example, that while a mother is nursing her babe she must take care not to work too hard because if her milk becomes "turbulent and hot" it can make the baby sick. This is strikingly similar to the Igorot belief, common in India as well, that if a mother gives her baby the breast while perspiring or agitated, it can cause the baby to have diarrhea.

Right or wrong, these beliefs focus on the mother and the importance of her physical well-being. Such cultural practices give her a feeling she is cared for and her baby is safe. This attention from others helps her relax, undoubtedly enhancing the milk ejection reflex.

When I was in Seni, I was most curious to find out where people believed the milk was "produced." Several said it was made in the breasts, but some older women contradicted them, suggesting it was manufactured in the upper chest and shoulder region. "We know this," one said, "because we can feel it coming down from there." She was referring to the sensations of fullness and flow that accompany the tingling sensations of the ejection or let-down reflex.

Anna and her mother had no doubts about the value of breastfeeding. "The baby is healthier," Anna said, "and the mother is more tranquil. She is certain that the baby has good food." Asunta recalled that she breastfed all her babies for two years except the oldest. When her firstborn was 18 months old she developed painful, bleeding nipples, so she stopped breastfeeding and gave the child goat milk. Anna also had a problem breastfeeding her first baby. After just four months her breasts became swollen and sore; she ran a temperature, and her milk supply began to dwindle. Just as her mother had done, Anna changed to goat milk; she diluted it with water and fed it to the baby with a bottle. She also gave him biscuits, bits of bread, and soft cheese and soup from a spoon.

The situation in these goatherding villages is unusual. Not

only is there vast knowledge about lactation throughout the culture, but goat milk is constantly available if a mother has difficulty or an inadequate supply.

Anna felt that her babies were especially vulnerable to illness when they were teething. At such times mothers worry more about *intossicazione* (the literal translation in Italian is "poisoning" or "intoxication," but Elizabeth believes Anna meant gastroenteritis). The women know that a baby can die within a day or so from severe diarrhea and vomiting. For this serious illness, they feed the child the liquid from cooked foods, especially apples, and little else. Mother's milk, they say, is "too heavy," and the baby shouldn't have much of it. Of course, the important thing is to get liquids into the baby to prevent dehydration. The World Health Organization has recently initiated a worldwide rehydration program that prescribes frequent feedings during diarrhea of a mixture of water, salt and sugar. Millions of babies have been saved by this simple potion.

The shepherd women, as with the mothers in the Philippines, report that teething usually coincides with the end of breastfeeding. However, even babies who continue getting some breastmilk are vulnerable at this time unless they have enough other foods. Remember, after the first three months, the breastmilk supply is no longer sufficient to maintain the child's normal growth pattern.

In this culture most mothers agree that they should give up breastfeeding once they become pregnant. They say it is dangerous not to do so. Anna and Asunta added that when a woman becomes pregnant, her milk changes. It looks different, which proves, they said, that something is wrong with it.

Many women do claim that their breastmilk grows lighter in color when they become pregnant. They accept it as a natural response to nutritional and hormonal changes. In Sardinia today, where most women are adequately nourished, a pregnant mother might be able to sustain her health, a foetus, and a breastfed baby in this "intimate triad" and none of the three would suffer. However, the conviction that pregnancy and breastfeeding are a bad combination has led to taboos that proscribe against intercourse—undoubtedly serving as protection for the mother especially when the diet is inadequate.

Sardinians call the milk produced by a pregnant woman *collostro* because they say it looks like the colostrum the breasts produce immediately after birth. Some believe it's poisonous to the child. An infant breastfed by a pregnant mother is referred to as *collostrato*. The women say that because such babies are thin and yellow others can tell the mother is pregnant and breastfeeding when she should not be.

Sardinian women state publicly that a mother who has intercourse and conceives while lactating is considered selfish. They are very reluctant to speak about sexual matters in public. Alone with Elizabeth, they explained that it was all right for a couple to have intercourse throughout a pregnancy, but they were expected to abstain for forty days after the birth. The abstinence was necessary, the women reasoned, because otherwise a mother might develop an infection. If a man was unwilling to do this, it was proof he didn't respect his wife. Nevertheless, it was the mother who was held responsible for a *collostrato*. It is common for the woman to be blamed—or praised—for the conception of a child, for its gender, for its personality traits, and for the state of its health. Many traditional cultures absolve the male completely, reinforcing the primacy of the mother. But it is a double-edged sword. (Recently, a report from China described a husband beating his wife when their child was the "wrong" sex.)

During her time in Seni, Elizabeth was often invited to have dinner with Asunta and her family. Their home, like most others in Seni, was a two-story stone dwelling, the ground floor taken up by a roomy kitchen with a stone stairway leading to sleeping quarters above. Outside there was a courtyard and a *cantina*—a storage room—attached to the house, where barrels of home-made wine were packed tightly together on wooden supports and jars of home-made tomato sauce were lined up on high shelves. There were also two stalls, kept very clean, for the family donkey and goat.

One night ten people, including Elizabeth, crowded into Asunta's house for evening dinner: Asunta and her 76-year-old husband; Anna and her two children; Maria Angela, the other daughter, and her son; Asunta's son, Mario, 30, who had the long torso and short legs typical of the men of the region; and her stepdaughter, Teresa, a tiny, extremely talkative woman in her forties who had never married.

Teresa was known as a gossip and a born troublemaker, but she was a lively person, full of opinions and ideas. Elizabeth learned that she had a low opinion of women. "They are not as intelligent as men," she said. "Women have *testi di gallini* (chicken heads). They run around doing a lot of work but their work isn't worth much." When Elizabeth objected, Teresa insisted, "Work that brings money into the house is worth a lot. If it doesn't bring money, it is of little value."

Dinner was *cordo*, a traditional Sardinian dish: the women stuff veal liver and kidneys into a length of intestine, wrap it with more intestine, and broil it on a rotating skewer over a wood fire in the kitchen fireplace. As usual it was served with wine and home-made bread.

Mario and his father unself-consciously joined the discussion of breastfeeding, relating it in a very down-to-earth way to their experience as shepherds. Neither had any doubt that mother's milk was best. Mario observed "When we have to bottle-feed a baby goat—even with the milk of another goat—it doesn't grow well."

Today in Seni most of the shepherds are older men. In 1976 the village included four or five families who owned enough land to be relatively well off, ten families with stores or small businesses, about 50 who merely subsisted by farming their own rocky, dry, infertile land, and 80 shepherd families. The rest of the villagers were either day laborers or old and retired. (Retired men often settled into a relatively sedentary old age; though the women work in their vegetable gardens until they are well into their seventies.)

The shepherds of Seni were better off in 1976 than they had been for many years since the meat and dairy products they produced were now in demand and brought in good money. However, those who had flocks of sheep had an advantage over the goatherders like Mario and his father because the sheepherders owned the pastures. In fact, they, together with the farmers, owned most of the land for about 20 miles around the village and were gradually fencing it in. The goatherders, formerly free to roam anywhere, now had to pay rent for pastures and competed fiercely for the less scrubby hills and those closer to the village.

The shepherds of Seni work long hours and spend most nights with their flocks. They have little margin of safety from natural calamities. Many animals are lost yearly to disease or prowling foxes. Few young men today are willing to live with such uncertainties. Most would prefer to emigrate to the continent and look for jobs. There was a major migration in the flourishing 1960s but after the oil embargo in 1973 the job market slumped in northern Italy and West Germany where most of them had found work. Jobless and unwanted they returned home. To make matters worse, these men now have trouble finding wives because young women will no longer accept the heavy, tedious work required of a shepherd's wife.

Paolo, Maria Angela's ten-year-old son, told Elizabeth he didn't want to be a shepherd when he grew up. The shepherds' wives are very firm; they want their children to have an easier life than they had. They believe education is the answer.

Fifty years ago the school system in Seni ended with the third grade, so most of the older villagers are hardly literate. Then, as now, children were absorbed into the family work system at an early age. By the time they are six, little girls like Anna's daughter are running errands and helping their mothers. Boys are allowed more time, since it takes a great deal of physical strength to be a shepherd or a farmer; though some are sent out with the goats at nine or so, most don't start working until they are eleven or twelve.

Today some of these patterns are changed. The local school goes through the eighth grade, and after that the students must take the bus to another village, 35 minutes away, to attend high school. Children still work alongside their parents, but most families hope to see their youngsters finish high school; a few whose families are better off even plan for college.

The continent still exerts a strong pull on the young of Seni, but so do the towns on the island's coast. Teenagers complain

that there's "nothing to do" in the village, but the older and
more traditional villagers say it's better to live in Sardinia
where at least a family can grow what they need to eat.

It's said that those who have seen Sardinia may suffer ever
after from *mal de Sardinia*—an incurable longing to return to
the island. Elizabeth, the anthropologist, has this malady. She
has gone back again and again. "There's a bittersweet quality
that draws you," she said. "The land is cruel—high, rocky, very
dry, very cold in winter—but it's incredibly beautiful."

Anna and her family are still very much rooted in traditional values and the old way of life. Graziella is a more modern woman. Her sister, Angela falls somewhere in between.

In 1976 Angela was 35 and the mother of three children, ages
3, 6 and 13. Stockier than her sister, she was married to a
prosperous shepherd and lived in a three-story version of the
typical Baru stone house. Like Anna she had an *orto*, but because the family could afford to buy some vegetables she had
a smaller garden and spent less time cultivating it.

Angela breastfed her first baby for a year. Since he didn't
gain weight satisfactorily she worried about him and whether
or not her milk was adequate. When he was 3 months old, she
tried giving him vegetable broth and biscuits but he refused
them. She fretted, and one day, a month later, her breasts
seemed to dry up. An elderly aunt told her someone must have
given her the evil eye and took her to a man who performed a
ritual to undo the damage. Angela recalled, "It worked so fast
that as I was leaving his house, even before I got out the door,
I could feel the milk flowing back down into my breasts."

How like the syndrome described by urban mothers in the
West where days of no support lead to feelings of insecurity
and stress which quickly result in the inhibition of the ejection reflex, and no milk. It is a vicious cycle. The hungry baby
cries and the mother's anxiety increases. As she becomes
frantic, fearing her milk will dry up, she has less and less
chance that her milk will let-down. The introduction of a supportive person, a doula, can have a dramatic effect; the cycle
is interrupted and the reflex functions.

She continued to breastfeed for eight months longer, but the

13. The author relaxes with a group of women in a Sardinian shepherd mountain community. "We had a lot of good laughs."

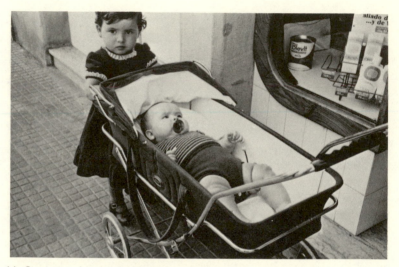

14. One generation ago the ideal image was a plump baby, but those lucky ones were usually from rich families. Now that weaning foods are readily available and affordable, infants are often overfed and overweight.

baby gained very little weight. He was still unwilling to take foods other than breastmilk, yet he seemed perpetually hungry. "He slept with me and was always at my breast, night and day," she recalled. "I had to stay at home all the time."

By the time the baby was a year old, Angela was very worried. She admitted to Elizabeth that he weighed only six or seven kilos—13 to 15 pounds. "I decided to wean him so that he would eat other things," she said. She followed the Sardinian practice and put a piece of sheep's wool over her breasts which frightened the baby. "He didn't eat anything for one week," she recalled. "I was scared. Then he began to take broth, potatoes, meat, the food of the family." And he gained weight.

While describing women in the Philippines, I mentioned research showing that the amount of breastmilk women produce under normal conditions increases to match the baby's needs only for the first few months. By three months, the average woman in these studies had reached a maximum volume and their milk leveled off. At six months, the supply tended to decrease in volume (Rowland et al. 1981). If the infant is not given additional foods, he will stop growing. This seems to be what happened to Angela's son. Even if he was having bits of foods other than breastmilk, it wasn't enough; his growth was stunted, and he was clearly undernourished. Some babies do not care much for foods other than milk, and some mothers, especially with their first child, are less experienced in coaxing them to eat. I remember one 2 year old in Trinidad who was so small he looked barely one year old. The child refused to eat for anyone except his father. When Papa came home for lunch, the child sat on his lap and nibbled from his hand.

Angela's second son was born in a hospital in northern Italy after her husband took a job in Turin. She recalled that the hospital staff insisted on giving the baby water in a bottle for the first three days after birth. They told her that colostrum wasn't good for an infant since it was yellow! (It is creamy-looking, compared to breastmilk.)

Angela's mother came to Turin just before the baby was born and stayed with her for a month afterward—a perfect doula arrangement. Breastfeeding was successful for three months, but then Angela's milk dried up. She gave the baby cow milk in a bottle, supplemented with broth and biscuits soaked in milk. At 12 months of age this baby weighed a healthy 24 pounds.

After eight years in Turin, the family returned to Baru, their mountain home. Most Sardinian emigrants then working on the continent sent money home or saved as much as possible so that they could return to their village and buy a bar, a shop, or livestock. Once home in Sardinia, Angela's husband bought sheep with the money he'd saved and became one of the more prosperous shepherds in the village.

The couple's third child, a daughter, was born in Baru with a midwife attending. Angela's sister, Graziella, stayed with her during the labor and delivery. Because their mother had died a year earlier, an older sister came to live with Angela for a while after the birth and was her doula.

As before, she planned to breastfeed the baby; but this time she developed cracked, painful nipples after just a month, so she gave up and switched to cow milk diluted with bottled water.

Though she took it for granted that a mother should breastfeed, Angela had some ambivalent feelings about it, as many mothers today do. She explained to Elizabeth, "I like to breastfeed because it's good for the baby, but it ages a woman— it dries her out. It's a sacrifice. For this reason girls today don't want to give the breast."

One day Elizabeth was present during a heated argument between Graziella, Angela, and their younger sister, Maria. Maria argued that, though breastmilk is good for the first three months of a baby's life, after that powdered milk is better. Graziella disagreed. She insisted it was because of powdered milk that Maria's baby developed diarrhea at the age of four months and had to be hospitalized. But Maria was stubborn. When she had her next baby, she said she would breastfeed if she could for three months *at most*, then switch to cow milk in a bottle. "If that doesn't work," she said, "I'll buy the powdered milk from the pharmacy again."

All three women agreed that breastmilk is the best food for a baby, at least in the beginning. But, in this same family, one sister (Angela) would breastfeed as long as possible, another (Maria) for three months but then she would move on to a product she thought was better, while the third (Graziella) was in such conflict after "not having enough milk" for her first baby that she did not try to breastfeed the next two. Each woman's pattern was unique not only from the other but also from those described by the older women in the community.

In traditional societies, where a woman has no alternative but to breastfeed because other forms of milk are not available or affordable, mothers must persevere no matter what if the baby is to survive. We still do not know how many cases of failure to breastfeed (and death of the infant) are culturally determined or how many are due to physiological malfunction. In every culture in the HLC study, some mothers reported problems such as cracked nipples, mastitis, and—most critical—insufficient milk.

In Sardinia today, when a baby is not growing—as Graziella's did not—the mother can resort to some other type of milk. In fact, because the villagers are a herding people, they have always had that option, though not all babies survive.

However, though other milk is available, the option to use it is not the only reason mothers in these Sardinian villages are breastfeeding for fewer months. Gradually, the extended family is shrinking, marriages are becoming more partner-centered, and there are new patterns to male-female relationships. The work women perform has changed and they have a new awareness of themselves in a world wider than just home and hearth.

For many of us it it tempting to idealize the pastoral life of the Sardinian shepherd villages, to mourn the good old ways and great old days and decry modern "corrupting" changes, including the relative "decline of breastfeeding." We must resist the temptation to blame it all on Western materialism.

The preoccupation with health care and family planning in Western countries has made the world a safer place for children, so that women today can afford to reach out, to extend their boundaries. They can hope for a more stimulating life; there's a new world out there now—the towns, the movies, the dances, the salary-paying jobs. The young women resist the old patterns, the way it used to be when mother worked so hard and looked so old. And breastfeeding was part of that old life.

Where women do have a real choice about infant feeding, *they do what they want to do and then find rationalizations to* justify their point of view. For example, when the anthropologist asked nursing mothers in her shepherd village why they chose to breastfeed, they told her that it was the natural way, it made the affections flow, it provided the baby with immunities. Women who preferred the bottle, on the other hand, explained that they found breastfeeding painful, or they did not have enough milk, or believed that, on the bottle, babies grow better and faster. Breastfeeders are convinced that nursing the baby keeps a woman young; bottle-feeders know very well that breastfeeding "drains" the mother!

In the mountains of Sardinia, as elsewhere, many different factors influence a woman's decision to breastfeed. She is affected by what she believes is best for the child's health; by how the baby is or is not growing; by how comfortable or complex it is for her to breastfeed, work and carry on the rest of her life; by how much she counts on nursing to delay her next pregnancy; by how much her family and community support her during this sensitive period—her matrescence; and, even by whether or not she enjoys breastfeeding. She is also influenced by powerful social pressures from her friends and family and by economic factors—can she afford to breastfeed or can she afford not to? All things considered, how a woman feeds is determined by what works best for her and maximizes her well-being.

In communities like Baru or Seni, where children are not malnourished and infant mortality is low, where there's money, refrigeration, and plenty of sheep milk, goat milk, and even commercial formula, it is hardly surprising that many mothers choose to breastfeed for only a few months or not at all.

5

ST. KITTS

More than half of the mothers in Rocky Point, a village on St. Kitts in the West Indies, were unmarried in 1976. Many were in their teens and too poor to stay home and take care of a child. Very often these teenage mothers had to manage alone right after childbirth if there were no close relatives in the area to whom they could turn for advice and support. Unemployment in the village and opportunities on other islands or in the United States attracted immigrants but also reduced the number of kin in the area that one could count on.

That was the situation when anthropologist Judy Gussler returned to this tiny village that year to conduct her fieldwork for the HLC study. She reported that the women breastfed for only a few months—a far shorter period than the mothers of any culture we've discussed so far. Yet, since so many lacked close kin, she was interested in discovering how it was they did so well.

Rocky Point is four miles outside of Basseterre, the capital of St. Kitts. Built on a hillside, it's a conglomeration of unpainted wooden houses, some no bigger than shacks, and larger, more attractive houses made of cement blocks that were stuccoed and painted in light colors.

Here and there in the village, fences made of wood, corrugated metal, or "trash" (sugar cane stalks) provide tiny yards with a semblance of privacy. Actually the houses are squeezed close together and the walls are so flimsy that in order to live together people insulate themselves against sights and sounds by putting themselves in a frame of mind anthropologists call "cultural blindness" or "cultural deafness."

In 1976 the village had street lights but no sewage system. A large number of families could not afford electricity and many of those who could had been waiting years to have their houses hooked up to the electric power lines. Very few homes had running water or an indoor toilet; most had an outhouse. At night in the yards goats mingled with pigs and chickens. In fact, goats were everywhere in St. Kitts: tethered to posts around the marketplace, grazing in parks in Basseterre where they sometimes sat on the park benches, wandering the unpaved alleys of Rocky Point, and helping to keep the place clean by munching the garbage in the gutters.

Rocky Point had a population of about 600. Half of the adult villagers, the luckier ones, had work in the sugar cane fields. Women usually do the weeding, and men cut cane with a machete—an exhausting task that nobody enjoys. (By the end of a cutting season in Jamaica, a period that lasts six to nine months a year, a man often weighs 25 percent less than when he started.)

Hard work aside, Rocky Point is a lively place with a rich verbal and musical culture. Music and dance, teasing, courting, and sexual experiences play an important part in the people's lives. Saturday night dances are held around the island at churches and community centers and at an old hotel outside the capital. Calypsonians are usually recruited from the area, but for fiestas, bands are brought in from the other islands. In Rocky Point the young people get dressed up—the women in slacks or jeans and high-heeled shoes—and most of them put in an appearance at a dance sometime between 10:00 P.M. and midnight. The festivities go on for most of the night; everyone dances and seems to have a good time. The gaiety is punctuated by loud insults hurled back and forth by the men at one another in a verbal game that is intended to produce fits of laughter from the onlookers. Occasionally this verbal sparring can sound all too real, alarming the spectators. In the

U.S. black community it's called "playing the dozens," and the opponents show off their verbal skills, demonstrate their self control and enhance their reputation within the community.

St. Kitts was once a British colony, and during the 17th and 18th centuries the owners of its sugar plantations imported slaves from Africa to work the cane. Gradually, most of the small farms owned by whites were absorbed into the sugar estates, whose owners often lived in England enjoying their wealth, while overseers ran their estates on the island. By the time the slaves were freed in 1833, the island population was almost entirely poor and black. It still is.

Since at the time of emancipation almost all the good agricultural acreage belonged to the plantations, the freed slaves had very limited access to the land. They remained dependent on the big sugar estates as they settled villages such as Rocky Point and planted gardens on inhospitable hillsides, the only sites available.

Little has changed. Kittitians still depend on the estates, though these lands have been nationalized by the island government. Theirs is virtually a single crop economy, with most food imported from outside. As we mentioned, jobs are scarce and many young people either emigrate to find work or else rely on some strong tie to someone who has left the island, found a job, and is willing to send money home. Emigration and finding a job overseas has become increasingly difficult.

Younger men can seldom adequately support a family, thus only half the adults ever marry and those who do often wait until they are in their 30s or 40s. But married or not, once a man fathers a child, he is supposed to support that child, in fact, the law requires it, and though fathers contribute, it is usually a minimal amount.

Marriage, home and family are the societal ideals, but real life does not work that way. No one praises an unmarried girl who becomes pregnant, but no one is shocked either. So, the normal pattern in St. Kitts is for girls to have their first baby at 15 or 16, and for 90 percent of first babies (and 75 percent of all babies) to be born to unmarried mothers. A girl begins to feel like a woman, not when she finds a job or marries but when she becomes a mother. And, even more accurate, as it was explained to me, "A girl has one baby; a woman has two."

Joyce was 29 years old in 1976. A rather small, slender woman with a deep voice and a round face, she wore her hair cropped short and, try as she might to straighten it, it refused to lie flat. She was an attractive woman in a community where many women already looked old by the time they were 29 or 30 because they were either gaunt or overweight or they had lost so many teeth.

Joyce was quite reserved (As Judy put it, "Kittitians are not a very huggy people."), but she was so animated that her energy gave her an air of self-confidence. She was the mother of five sons, ages from one-and-a-half to 12 and she was pregnant again. She lived with Clement, the father of her last two sons, in a weathered, unpainted, wood-frame house that had no electricity or plumbing—there was an outhouse in the yard.

The house was typical of many in Rocky Point. Its living room was about six by seven feet and was furnished with a couple of straight-backed wooden chairs. The only other room was slightly larger, contained two beds, and Joyce, Clement, and the five children all slept there. The kitchen was in a shed in the yard, and since there was no table in the house the family ate sitting on the porch steps.

Joyce was born in Rocky Point and had lived there all her life, except for a couple of weeks she once spent on St. Croix looking for a job. She attended a local one-room school until sixth grade. At 16 she became pregnant for the first time. It was a hard pregnancy, and she often felt weak and dizzy. A doctor finally told her she had low blood pressure. When it was time for the baby to be born, she went into a hospital in Basseterre. (It was so overcrowded that beds had been set up in the hallways, but it was still less crowded than one hospital I saw during a site visit in Jamaica. There two women and their babies shared every bed, lying head to foot.)

Joyce's baby weighed only four pounds at birth, though they say he was full term. She wasn't able to breastfeed him—perhaps because she had been sick. She told Judy, "I didn't seem to have much milk." She didn't know much about breastfeeding anyway, because women in St. Kitts seldom talk about it. "Most of what I know about breastfeeding I read in books," Joyce explained. Other mothers said they learned from the medical staff at the hospital. In fact, the women of Rocky Point were so close-mouthed about breastfeeding that Judy guessed some of them may still fear the effects of evil spirits. In the old days, she was told, people almost never discussed a pregnancy, a birth, or a new baby lest the "jumbies"—the spirits of the dead—hear them and cause the infant to sicken and die. (It is somewhat comparable in Western cultures to a fear that one is tempting fate to talk about how well things are going, so when that taboo is broken, we knock on wood.)

When she got out of the hospital, Joyce returned to her mother's house, where she had lived before the baby was born. She stayed there until she became pregnant again just three months later. The second pregnancy so soon angered her mother Estelle, who told her she would have to move out. Estelle's response is somewhat predictable since it is common for a girl to move out when she is pregnant for the second time.

Joyce's third son was born in 1967 when she was 19 years old. All three had the same father. He gave her money and clothes for the children from time to time, but he never lived with her and eventually he left St. Kitts. Estelle moved to St. Croix early in the 1970s and after that she also sent money home.

Joyce's grandmother, who was still living in Rocky Point, gave her some help with the babies. Providing for them was hard. Once Joyce took a job as a domestic at a small local hotel for about $7.50 a week, but she had trouble finding anyone she could trust with whom to leave her babies. In addition, they were often sick. "You come home and meet your baby sick," she recalled, "and still have to go out and leave it and it's getting worse every day. And you can't take time out to carry it to a doctor." The frustration, fear, and guilt she felt are all too familiar to working mothers everywhere.

For a while Joyce left the boys with their father's mother. One day she came home and found that one of them had been badly burned with an iron. Sometimes she tried leaving the children with her sister. Though she left food for them, she would come back in the evening and find they had not eaten all day. Her sister said they simply were not hungry, but as soon as Joyce got home they clamored for food.

By late 1970 she had reached the point where she would feed the children in the morning, then lock them in the house for the day to keep them safe. She said the older youngsters, now 5 and 6 years old, could find the "tea" for themselves (in St. Kitts "tea" means almost any type of hot drink) and they had toys to play with. At that time, Joyce had "taken up with" Clement. He was a tall man, good-looking despite the fact that he was missing a number of teeth—he'd learned to smile without opening his mouth. (Dental decay is rampant throughout the West Indies, to the point where some of my Jamaican informants spoke warmly about how good it was when the groom's family gave the bride dentures as a wedding present.)

Since Clement was unemployed, he would stop in and check on the boys from time to time during the day. His visits were considered a very kind gesture indeed. Kittitian males might willingly support their own children, but most prefer not to become too involved with the children their woman had by another man.

After they lived together for a time, Clement kindly agreed to keep Joyce's sons while she went to St. Croix to look for work. Her grandmother took care of them during the day and Clement was with them at night. However, after just a few weeks, Joyce came home again. She found St. Croix too big and the pace too fast for her—and she missed her children very much.

Joyce breastfed all but her first baby, starting, as most Kittitian mothers do, after the milk came in on about the third day. She said the local doctors, who advise women to breastfeed while their babies are small, had explained that it gave the children "immunities."

With her second son Joyce breastfed for nine months and then stopped because she was pregnant again. The women of St. Kitts say that it is not a good idea to continue breastfeeding once a mother is pregnant, though when Judy Gussler asked them why not, they had no explanation. Joyce's third son was breastfed for a year and two months; with the fourth she had to stop after six months when he went into the hospital for a hernia operation. But she nursed her fifth baby until he was 14 months old, a very long time in St. Kitts. Most young mothers told Judy they stopped after six or seven months, and they giggled and joked in a somewhat embarrassed way at the idea that a baby over nine months might still be on the breast. Joyce explained that she finally had to wean this last baby because he kept waking her at night to nurse and constantly asked for the breast, even in public, which embarrassed her. Kittitian women seldom breastfeed in public.

Few infants in St. Kitts are *totally* breastfed beyond the age of about two weeks, and Joyce's babies were no exception. Almost from the time they were born, she regularly gave her sons milk in a bottle, along with breastmilk. She made it from evaporated milk, diluted with boiled water and stored in a thermos.

Ordinarily in Rocky Point a mother begins bottle-feeding shortly after she gets home from the hospital, and the usual routine is to breastfeed morning and evening and use the bottle during the day. Though the milk is expensive, mixed feeding is actually a practical solution. Even if a woman does not have a regular job—and most do not—she works from time to time and has to be ready to go out to work at a moment's notice when an opportunity arises. That means having a baby who won't fuss when given a bottle.

In many families a young mother's earnings help to support not only her children, but also her mother, her mother's younger children, and perhaps an out-of-work brother. Her breadwinner's role means that some women must emigrate just a few months after giving birth, leaving the children behind in the care of their mother or grandmother. Of course, these babies are bottle fed. (The situation seems very similar to what I saw on other islands, where many young women have one foot on the home island and the other on a plane to the United States.)

Mixed feeding is the most common tradition in this region, and the general feeling is that even for a small baby breastmilk isn't enough. Asked why they began giving a bottle, women told Judy, "My baby wasn't satisfied and I had to feed him more," or simply, "He needed more to grow on." When asked why they stopped breastfeeding after six or seven months, most women said it was because they hadn't enough milk. Many are convinced their breastfeeding problems stem from inadequate nourishment. They are sure that Kittitians were stronger and healthier in the past.

In 1976 ads in movie theaters and on radio for baby formula had little effect on the island custom of combining bottle and breastfeeding, possibly because most women could not afford formula. About 75 percent used evaporated milk, while those who found even evaporated milk too expensive fed "bush tea." They picked leaves from particular bushes or trees, dried them, and steeped them in hot water to make a tea, then added as much evaporated milk as they could afford.

Joyce began giving her babies soft foods (*beikost*) as soon as they were a month old. (Many women wait two months.) She used either prepared baby cereal or a porridge she made by mixing a teaspoon of corn meal with evaporated milk, boiled water, and a small amount of sugar. She made up six ounces of porridge in the morning, stored it in a thermos, and gave it to the baby in a bottle twice a day. In Rocky Point corn meal porridge is often the main item in a child's diet for the first year or two of life. Joyce began offering her babies mashed pumpkin and white potato once they were about 4 months old.

A mild degree of malnutrition is not uncommon in Rocky Point, but it is more often a problem with 1 and 2 year olds; infants have a fairly adequate diet. Judy discovered that about half the babies on the whole island weighed somewhat less than is normal for their age. Despite this, they received enough additional foods so they were able to cope with the insults from the environment. In fact, the infant mortality rate in St. Kitts was half what it was in most developing countries.

A number of factors combine to make toddlers the age group most likely to be undernourished. First, many mothers feel their children are too young to need "relish" (meat or fish). Some believe it is bad for them; others cannot offer it because they are too poor. Even the adults eat only a small amount.

Second, many toddlers don't yet have their own bowl, fork, and spoon. In St. Kitts poor people don't buy a whole set of dishes or cutlery; they invest in such items only as each child becomes old enough to need them. Result: toddlers take their milk, juice, and porridge from a bottle. When the rest of the family eat, they simply offer the little one food to taste from their own plate, and no one really keeps track of what and how much the child eats. Weight increases as soon as the child is old enough to take a portion from the family pot or join the older children drifting through the village, occasionally stealing fruit from the trees and gardens.

Judy reminded us that health professionals believe frequent diarrhea is partly to blame for the poor nutritional state of some children, since diarrhea drains the body and prevents the digestive system from absorbing nutrients. Joyce's fourth son had rusty hair, a sign symptomatic of malnutrition. He had diarrhea at that time and was being treated for worms; both conditions certainly contributed to his weakened state.

The water in Rocky Point is relatively clean and safe; still babies get diarrhea often. Judy reported that the real problem is not the water, but (as in Sagada) the contaminated environment. The village had open drains, and flies, animals and animal excrement were everywhere.

Several times, Judy brought her children with her to St. Kitts on field trips. She recalled that for the first two days of the first of these trips she boiled all the household water. She stopped when she realized " . . . I wasn't going to get any research done because I was spending all my time boiling water—for drinking, for ice cubes, for Kool-Aid and everything else." Her son developed gastroenteritis within a month, but her two older girls had no problems. Judy recalled that during their stay every cut the children got, every blister, every pimple seemed to become infected. When living in poverty and in a tropical environment, everything takes longer to do; one becomes accustomed to waiting for jobs, taxis, people, doctors and cures.

By American standards, few people in Rocky Point have a sufficient diet. Adults and older children typically begin the day with a breakfast of bread and a hot drink, such as tea. Lunch or dinner is bread with a little sausage or cheese, if the family can afford it, and a cold drink. Supper might be a bit of "relish" with rice or dumplings and perhaps some starchy vegetable. Though women tend to grow stout on this diet, the men remain lean.

The villagers often joked about special "strengthening food" that was supposed to help prepare one for work, sex, or a lively Saturday night. Once, when Judy was observing a cooking class, a young woman was meekly rolling out some dough when her friend chided her, insisting she had not had her "goat water" on Saturday night. Goat water is mutton stew. Coconut water is strengthening, and so is conch—harvested from the beach and simmered for a very long time. The saying goes, "Conch will help you get more children."

Local tradition does not include special foods for women who are pregnant or breastfeeding, yet there are certain foods breastfeeding mothers are *not* supposed to eat, such as mangos, avocados, sugar cane, and sugar cakes. The women say that they are hungrier than usual while pregnant or lactating, but they can rarely afford to buy extra food.

Food and rent ate up virtually all of the income in most households in 1976. Joyce also had no money to spare. She depended mainly on the $15 a week that Clement contributed after he found a job as a truck driver. In addition, the father of her first three sons regularly gave her clothes for his children and every two months or so sent her some money. Once or twice a year she made a little extra income by selling surplus sweet potatoes she had grown or a pig she had raised. She said that as soon as the new baby was born, she would have to look for work again.

On a typical day, Joyce got up at dawn, about 5:00 A.M., to get her household organized and the children off to school. Like other mothers in the community, she made sure her kids were well-scrubbed, with their shoes shined and their shirts freshly ironed—despite the fact that her house had no running water or electricity. Once the boys were gone, her first task of the day was usually the laundry. She couldn't afford to buy much clothing for herself or the boys—most members of the family owned just two outfits—and so she had to wash every day if they were to have something clean to wear.

Before they left for school, the children fetched water in a

15. Kitchens in St. Kitts are in a shed in the yard. With no separate dining area, they eat outside sitting on the stairs.

16. A good present from a woman's man is a can of powdered milk for the weanling.

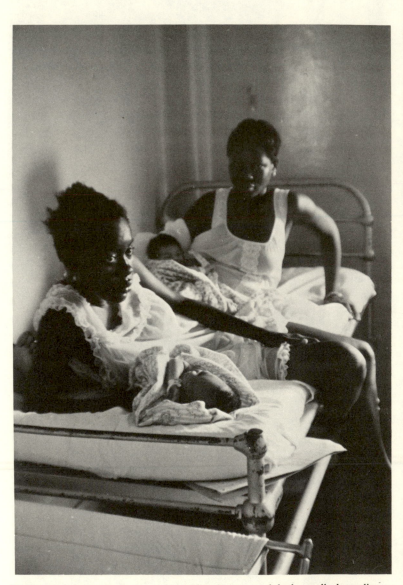

17. Hospitals in the developing world seldom have enough beds, medical supplies or surgical equipment or food. In Kingston, Jamaica two mothers and their babies share one bed in Jubilee hospital, which recorded 14,000 births in 1975.

galvanized tin bucket from the standpipes in the village street and poured it into a concrete trough in the back yard. Joyce did the laundry there with cold water and a bar of soap: She soaked the clothes, pounded them to beat out the dirt, and then hung them on a line to dry. (Most households had no clothes line, so the wet clothes were carefully draped over bushes or whatever else was handy and dust free.)

Like the majority of the villagers, Joyce patched together a piecemeal living; she had to be resourceful to survive. In the course of a day she might hear that some woman was ill and needed help with a garden, and so she'd go weed in return for some vegetables—perhaps potatoes; or she'd hear of a woman in the city who was looking for a domestic worker or a temporary babysitter and she'd take a bus into Basseterre to see about the job. Occasionally, someone in the village needed help "pulling" peanuts which grow underground and have to be up-rooted like onions or potatoes; by pulling peanuts she could earn about 50 cents a day. (Imagine, if you will, that she also has to breastfeed her newest baby—survival is her artistry.)

Joyce had other tasks that took her away from home. If someone in a nearby village had fish to sell, she would go and buy some for resale. Then again, after she and Clement had decided to enlarge their house, whenever she found a bit of time she would go to the seashore and collect a pile of rocks for the extension. Perched on top of the pile in the shade of a makeshift shelter she erected, she hammered the rocks into gravel. Eventually, she and Clement would mix the gravel with mortar to make cement for the addition.

Cooking was time-consuming and she was feeding seven, so Joyce started early in the day. Her stove was a coal pot, a metal container the size of a small bucket; she filled the bottom of it with charcoal, lit it, and set the pot of food on top. She could cook only one pot at a time. In better days, Joyce had used a two-burner kerosene stove, the way most people preferred to cook, but since the oil crisis in 1973 kerosene had been in short supply. On an island shortages occur frequently, and people are used to adjusting and making do.

After dinner, Joyce might take a walk around the streets for a while, but not too often because in Rocky Point it is not a

good thing for women to do if they care about their reputation. Since so few homes have electricity, even the men and
some of the "wilder" young girls who hang around the streets
are in by 10:00 P.M.

For women like Joyce, who have young children, the biggest
problem is having to leave the youngsters at home while they
go out to work. Most don't consider what they do as a "real"
job, even though they work every day, because, as Judy put it,
"Women have bought a whole bill of goods that 'work' is when
you draw a paycheck." However, the tasks that fill up Joyce's
day are not only essential to keep the family going but most
of them take her out of the house. Again, despite these pressures, so many mothers still manage to breastfeed.

In the early 1970s, Judy Gussler did a study of food-sharing
in Rocky Point that uncovered many facets about interper-
sonal relationships in the village. Her early interviews showed
that people do not share food outside the family. However, once
she got close to the women, she discovered that they frequently do give gifts of food not only to relatives but also to
friends, neighbors, or people with whom they work. In direct
contrast to the conspicuous way we give presents in Western
cultures, Kittitians are most circumspect, even secretive, careful
not to be seen, else others might be covetous. Food is expensive, and if someone is seen giving it out, others might try to
get some for themselves. As for the person receiving the food,
she would feel humiliated if people began to think of her as
someone needing help.

Gossip is an important form of social control and a fact of
life in Rocky Point. Joyce once explained to Judy that she
couldn't borrow a friend's maternity clothes because everyone
would say, "There goes Joyce, wearing Agatha's clothes."

Many of the people of Rocky Point are estranged from one
another, a common occurrence especially where families live
in very close proximity. This animosity can be long-lasting. Judy
observed she never came across anyone in the village who was
on speaking terms with everyone else. When she tried to follow the method we suggested of getting different generations
of women together in groups to talk about child feeding, she
found it difficult because most women couldn't think of more

than two or three friends with whom they would discuss intimate subjects such as breastfeeding.

Nevertheless, like most poor people throughout the world, the villagers are extremely dependent on one another to make ends meet. And yet, one doesn't see a lot of affect and touching. In fact, people tend to be more stern, strict, even harsh with each other and with their children. Without large family networks, most of their time and energy is spent on keeping their life together and food on their plate. Women try to maintain as extensive a support network as possible—ties with several different men and women, especially relatives, whom they can call on when they have no money, when they or their children are ill, when they need contributions towards a son's bail or when they bury a relative. However, given the nature of Kittitian emigration, these relationships are shifting and tenuous. But as a woman gets older, her grown children become her primary source of support, so she is lucky if she has several children to take care of her in her old age. On the other hand, since many women want to emigrate, in which case children would be a liability, a lot of ambivalence exists towards them. Yet when asked why they had their first children even though they knew it wold make life more difficult, women will say, "I wanted somebody to love." Children are the most stable feature in one's life.

Sarah, another good informant whom Judy came to know well, was only 18 and had not yet developed an adequate support network. Petite and quite pretty, she was already the mother of three children. Each had a different father, and at the time of this study none of them was helping her. Matthew, the father of the youngest child, had given her some financial support for a while, but she had heard nothing from him for six months. As we have pointed out, the law requires men to support their children, illegitimate or not, but many don't. However, some fathers indicate that they would be willing to help out if only they could earn enough money. The ideal is a job with sufficient earnings to take care of oneself and still contribute to two, or perhaps three households. Many do. In the village a woman who takes a man to court to get support—and few can afford to—will be severely criticized by other women as well as the men. In many ways men are dependent on women. In Jamaica I was told, "If a man have no woman to take him in, he sleep in the street." Such are the contradictions.

Sarah had no parents she could count on. Her mother and father both left St. Kitts when she was very young, abandoning their three children. For some years, she lived with a distant relative, but in 1972 his house burned down and she moved into a place of her own. A year later, when she was 15, her first child was born; within the next two years she had two more children.

Sarah's first baby was born in the hospital. She started to breastfeed, but soon developed an abscess and had to give it up. After that she bottle fed the baby with evaporated milk, diluted and sweetened with sugar. Her other two children were born at home with the help of a midwife. She breastfed the second for five months, the third for seven months.

In 1976 Sarah was recovering from an "illness." Other women in the village suspected she'd had an abortion, probably self-induced with a plant called "churchyard weed," a poison that causes severe abdominal contractions. Sarah was then living in a fly-ridden two-room shack with her 15-year-old cousin, the cousin's baby, and her own children. The cousin helped her when she was sick.

Sarah was desperate. Her youngest child was a year old and no longer breastfeeding. Her income averaged about $7 a week, and of that she figured she spent $1.40 a week to buy a large tin of powdered milk (not milk formula) for the children, that is, about a quarter of her food money—and one-fifth of her total income—went for milk. What's more, this tin of powdered milk would feed her three children for a week only if it were watered down.

Most of the women in the village had little use for Sarah. They said she ran around too much with men—she loved the Saturday night dances—and didn't take proper care of her children. Joyce occasionally gave her advice and helped her out because she was "something" (a distant cousin) to Clement, but even Joyce was impatient with her. In her notebooks, Judy described Sarah's babies as quite listless; the middle child had a distended abdomen and rusty hair, a bad sign, and was frequently sick. Judy could recall only one occasion when she saw Sarah take a child in her arms for feeding or comforting.

And yet she was no different than hundreds of others. She would manage. Once she was a little older, she would find a man who had a stable job; the affair would develop into a durable relationship and if she became pregnant, the man would help provide for her. That is the way this system works.

Understandably, Sarah didn't have any illusions about men. When Judy asked her if she'd like to have a man live with her, she said she would not because men are so fickle and untrustworthy. Her attitude was not uncommon among the women in Rocky Point.

Many women told Judy that they regretted giving up their independence to let a man move in with them. Men are traditionally dominant, and women are supposed to put up with their ways and their outside affairs. Wife-beating and girlfriend-beating are not unusual. Yet most of the women said they'd like to get married eventually, because marriage gave them better standing in the community.

But since marriage must be preceded by a steady job, it is unlikely to happen much before middle age. In the meantime, from the male point of view, in this community where a man cannot get his status from the work he does, he has little else to define himself other than his prowess as a lover and his paternity. So fathering children and having a woman who is pregnant adds to his status. The word "macho" is used to describe this attitude. It means "a real man."

Contradictory as it may seem, in some ways the women of Rocky Point are more fortunate than the men. They live longer, appear to be stronger and more secure, and they are employed. The young men, on the other hand, are jobless most of the time. Many of them continue to live with their mother or share a shack with other men sometimes with no kitchen—few know how to cook anyway. One of Judy's key informants was living in a tiny house with his father, his brother and another brother's two children. The women at least have their own house even when they are teenagers. Many houses are rented and there is a perpetual movement from one rented house to another. "People live as best they can," Judy explained.

Most children in St. Kitts know their biological father and even if he ignores them at first, as the years pass, he tends to develop a closer relationship, in fact, children provide many men with the only stable tie they have, since their affairs with women are generally tentative. A man who has established a close bond with his children is considered better off. At least he can count on his daughter to care for him in his old age and his son to contribute to his support. The bare facts are that only the mother, father and the grandparents have a real investment in the future of any child. When others help the parents it is on a mutual exchange basis but not from any expectation that the child will eventually help or support them.

The unwed teenage mothers of St. Kitts were not rebellious, wanton or loose. Rather, they were having babies and becoming adults in the only way available to them. An interesting study was conducted in Cincinnati with a group of couples who have the same domestic arrangement as in St. Kitts—unwed partners with a child. These young people were compared with middle class black married couples whose life script included a household arrangement before they had their child. When this latter group had a baby, it put an extraordinary strain on their relationship and they were far more likely to split up than couples who, though not married, relied on the mother's mother for help (Fairley 1981). Obviously, there is something in this pattern of social organization that functions well.

Judy went back to St. Kitts a number of times after the HLC study, most recently in 1981. She found that over the years, Joyce's lot in life improved. She now had a regular job as a maid at a tourist hotel.

Joyce's sixth child was a girl, and after this baby she began taking birth control pills. Judy asked her if she would consider sterilization, and she said no. At the time she was afraid that Clement might be about to leave her and, realist that she was, she knew that she had to remain capable of bearing children in case she needed to find another man to take his place and help support the family. Birth control programs have been hampered in St. Kitts because many women share Joyce's dilemma. Children, a great joy but obviously a financial liability, remain the only insurance a woman has against a destitute old age.

By 1981 Joyce and Clement had finished building the extension to their house. They had added two tiny rooms, each not much bigger than the bed it held, so now the whole family no longer had to sleep in one room. They even had the house wired for electricity, and Joyce's sister sent a refrigerator from St. Croix. Judy brought her a second-hand, black-and-white television as a gesture of affection and appreciation for her help during her fieldwork.

The village now had about a dozen TV sets—more televisions than telephones—and this influx of video culture was having one unexpected result. Suddenly Clement and other men, who'd been spending their evenings together hanging out on the streets of the village, began to stay home to watch TV. The women welcomed the change; for many it relieved that nagging sense of insecurity.

Sarah was not much better off than before, but at least she had not had any more babies. She worked for a while in a factory but found she couldn't afford to keep the job because of the high cost of bus fare and the shoes she had to buy to wear at work. (In Rocky Point an adult usually gets by with "draggers," inexpensive rubber thong sandals.) Eventually, Sarah found work weeding cane fields; it paid less than the factory job and was hot and back-breaking, but it was closer to home.

Once, when she was feeling particularly low, Sarah sat down and wrote a letter to Judy in the United States. Summing up her situation, she said:

Right now I am very broke . . . . Cant even get a job . . . . Its a lady living side me she cant walk so good it is she who do give me little change sometime to buy milk for (the babies) and when she dont give me they would drink the plain boiled water.

Some things have changed for breastfeeding mothers in St. Kitts over the years. Most significant, new babies are no longer bottle-fed in the hospital unless the mother can't breastfeed.

People in the health ministries around the world are newly aware of the benefits of breastfeeding and are concerned that it not decline. The government of St. Kitts has set up an educational program to inform women how they can breastfeed more successfully and to discourage unnecessary bottle feeding. Hence, the change in the hospital routine.

Judy, however, learned that the new insistence on breast-feeding was not working out as ideally as hoped. The babies were kept in the hospital nursery and were brought in to be breastfed only once every four hours. Meanwhile, the mothers could hear the infants crying and they were upset, wondering if their baby was one of those crying. Furthermore, though 98 percent of the mothers did breastfeed while in the hospital, once the women went home they did as they have always done—within two weeks 65 percent of them were giving the baby a bottle as well.

Once before, in the 1960s, the government made an attempt to promote breastfeeding, and the campaign failed. Such promotions will probably continue to have but a minimum success until this small island achieves a degree of prosperity that makes it possible for women to stay home and breastfeed if they like. *Government health workers list the island's biggest problems as infant health, infant nutrition, and birth control, but the women put it differently: They say what they need are jobs and additional food to feed their children.*

The HLC field studies in Jamaica and Trinidad report situations roughly similar to the one in St. Kitts. In a Jamaican village in 1976, one woman told me, "Sure, I breastfeed but I want a dress and some shoes too." She owned one dress, and there would be no money for another until she worked.

In Trinidad, another village in our study was settled by East Indians. All mothers breastfed, but they were eager to get their babies onto the bottle as early as possible so that the grandmothers could feed the children while they went back to work. Where women once filled the baby's bottle with a solution of sago or tapioca, some now use evaporated milk or imported formula. Nutritionally, the change is an improvement, but it also creates a problem: Formula has to be mixed with local water. No natural water supply exists in the village, and sometimes the weekly water trucks are delayed and the only water left is at the bottom of the tanks. As the water level sinks, bacteria thrive. "When the tanks get low, we all get sick a little," the patriarch of the community told me. Diarrhea for adults is distressful, but for infants, it is dangerous. Once the villagers complained to the town officials, and as a punishment, they were made to wait even longer.

In the shanty town in Kingston, Jamaica, where HLC anthropologist Ida Daum did her fieldwork, many of the young mothers were unmarried, as in St. Kitts. "Having a baby for many girls is often a crisis situation," Ida wrote.

They usually have to find a new place to live, think about supporting themselves and the child . . . . After the baby is around for a while and the mother finally begins to come out with him and people know about it, the father is more likely to begin supporting the child if they both stay in the same area. Sometimes, especially in the country . . . men run away, in shame of not being able to help, in shame of not being able to be a man.

Some mothers in Kingston did not breastfeed at all because they could not stay home with the baby. Ida noted that women, whether or not they had jobs, had to get out "to pursue various things needed to make life go on for the other children in the household." She said it was very clear that what the mothers fed their infants depended on how much money they had.

As in St. Kitts, virtually all women who breastfeed are also giving their babies some kind of additional food by the time they are two months old. They buy cow milk or formula if they can afford it. However, some have milk or formula in the house only when the child's father brings it as a gift, and the rest of the time they give the baby corn meal porridge.

In 1973 there was a milk shortage in Jamaica. One local doctor naively advised mothers, no matter what age their young, to cope with the shortage by breastfeeding! Even among health professionals, many did not understand that a woman with a 7-month-old infant (and a milk supply already dwindling or ended) could not meet her baby's nutritional needs by breastfeeding, even if she could relactate.

Most mothers continued to use bottles during the shortage but filled them with diluted corn meal porridge. Even nursing mothers with very young babies, who might have been able to increase their milk supply by breastfeeding day and night, followed a more natural pattern. They breastfed and used next-best substitutes as additional food. Besides corn meal porridge, women also tried bush and fish teas and sugar water, and later, when corn meal itself was in short supply, many replaced it with orange juice and strained oats. The mothers assumed the shortage would end, but in the meantime, they continued to mix-feed or bottle-feed, using whichever choice made their lives easier.

Many American mothers are convinced that mixed feeding won't work. They sincerely believe that a baby who is given a bottle will soon reject the breast because the milk flows more easily from a bottle, or they rationalize that mothers who try to combine bottle and breastfeeding are bound to give up breastfeeding rather quickly. The experience of mothers in Jamaica and St. Kitts, however, is that babies don't reject the breast when they're offered both breast and bottle. Remember the account from Zaire where over one-third of the mothers use mixed feeding for nine months to a year and then *discontinue* bottle feeding, substituting soft foods, while they continue to breastfeed (Franklin, 1982). Similarly, women in these West Indian communities breastfeed for less than nine months, yet they find mixed feeding compatible.

Ironically, the babies were in better health than babies in some traditional societies where mothers breastfed longer but without adequate supplements. Despite the fact that the evaporated milk was often overdiluted, the babies had enough other supplementary food so that, combined with breastfeeding, they fared fairly well.

Most Kittitian mothers never doubted that breastfeeding is best. They give the bottle as well, partly because they have to go out to work and partly because they have problems breastfeeding even in the beginning. Sometimes, though a woman's mother does act as her doula, she too has a day full of work and that can put strain on their relationship.

Asked why they began giving the bottle in the first place, over 60 percent of the mothers said they started when they felt there was not enough milk—a universal statement. Quite easily, they mixed beikost foods, breast- and bottle-feedings, while pursuing a multitide of other activities: playing with their babies, keeping their man happy, helping their mothers, and exchanging affection with sisters or friends.

Kittitian women are poor but not preoccupied with their poverty. Despite the fact that every day the major worry is how to get enough food for themselves and their family, their lives have diversity and laughter and personal visions of the good life—some attained, many unrealized.

6

THE UNITED STATES: URBAN MOTHERS

We U.S. mothers describe breastfeeding as an almost mystical happening—an experience that forges a unique bond between mother and child, a fulfillment that makes a woman feel like a woman in a way nothing else can. And, in but one decade, regardless of social class, this new-found joy and commitment, increased the incidence of breastfeeding several hundred percent.

Well then, if breastfeeding is so desirable why do such a high proportion of American women today still continue to bottle feed?

In 1982 private hospitals in the U.S. suburban communities reported that 52 percent of new mothers chose to bottle feed. In towns and cities the figure was even higher. According to a 1980 survey of women who gave birth in municipal hospitals in New York City (where most maternity patients are from lower-income families), 82 percent chose not to breastfeed. However, if we combine the private and municipal institutions, the average number of women breastfeeding was 32 percent—a remarkable change considering that a decade earlier only about 5 percent were breastfeeding.

Of course, there is no simple answer for the persistence of formula feeding but the sensitive qualitative data collected by the team of women anthropologists for the HLC study led to some important clues. For instance, their analyses, whether describing Mexican women in Houston, Cubans in Florida or market women in Nigeria showed us that a woman's decision to breastfeed was influenced by: the family's economic status, the mother's work outside the home, her anticipation of work (she must be ready when the jobs are offered), her access to substitute caretakers, her health, her energy level, the strength of her motivation, the health and personality of the baby—in other words, a myriad of factors, most of which were beyond her control. Consistently, one fact was apparent: the poorer the family the more limited the feeding choices available to her.

Similar factors, I discovered, control the choices made by poor American mothers. My fieldtrips with these mothers took me one steamy afternoon in August 1982 through a public housing project in Waterbridge, Connecticut, to meet Roberta, my first informant. The neighborhood has a reputation as dangerous. Three-story rundown brick buildings faced one another across treeless streets with many broken windows in the uninhabited ground floor apartments. There were few women in sight, but small groups of out-of-work men of all ages congregated on the sidewalks, some leaning back on wooden chairs propped against the buildings. Unemployment among the blacks and Hispanics in the city was high.

I talked to Roberta at the community center on the edge of the apartment project where she worked. A soft-spoken, handsome young black woman, she was dressed in a mauve blouse and white skirt and looked cool despite the heat. Roberta had gone to college for a year but dropped out when she got married. She had two children, a 5-year-old boy and a 6-month-old girl. With the first baby, she chose to breastfeed because she was convinced breastmilk was best for the baby and because "everyone was doing it," or so it seemed. Actually, she was the first of her friends to marry and have a baby and as we talked she surprised herself when she realized that none of them had breastfed. It turned out that her impressions about breastfeeding had come from her extensive reading about childbirth and breastfeeding. Her introduction to the subject she recalled came from a pamphlet which prompted her to ask her doctor for advice. She claimed she had no doula, but once the baby was born she got a lot of help from the books she read. She and her baby son settled down together with no real problems, and she breastfed for three months.

When her second baby was born, she decided not to breast-feed. Whether or not she thought it was best, the baby had formula from the beginning. She explained, "I wasn't eating well at the time. I had lost a lot of weight, so I didn't think the milk would be good for the baby." Breastfeeding would also be "a hassle," she reported. Besides, her husband would dis-approve if she breastfed in public, so she couldn't take the baby with her when she went out unless she brought along supple-mentary bottles.

"When I was nursing my son, I dripped all the time," she recalled, "and there was my husband's attitude to consider. Though he didn't seem to mind that I breastfed the first time, with this second baby he wasn't keen on it."

Roberta conveyed the impression that this time around nothing was as good as the first time. The baby wasn't planned, and her husband, a welder, had lost his job, so it was clear she would have to go back to work fairly soon after the birth. Help from relatives kept the family afloat but just barely. She may have hoped to fit breastfeeding into her life but with so much pressure on her it was fairly obvious she could not.

With limited funds, she had turned to the federal program known as WIC (the Special Supplemental Food Program for Women, Infants, and Children mandated by Congress) as a source for food stamps for herself and free formula for the baby.

Roberta said she would breastfeed again if she were to have another child. She still believes that it's best for the baby and apparently for her relationship with the baby. "I feel closer to my first child. My daughter is more attached to her father," she added.

I wasn't surprised to learn that she felt guilty about her re-lationship with her daughter and focused the blame on her decision not to breastfeed. "I don't like a lot of canned things myself," she explained. "And I've just realized I don't know what's in the cans of milk. There must be a lot of chemicals since it says on the label it has a shelf life of a year." I tried to reassure her that there was nothing dangerous in the can, but her regrets were so strong and tinged with guilt it didn't do much to alleviate her fear.

Roberta's honesty and her rationalizations helped her to do whatever she felt had to be done. Notice that in the case of the first baby, it "brought them closer" to each other and her husband "didn't mind." But when breastfeeding was not appropriate a few years later with a second child, she was getting "too thin" to breastfeed, it was a "hassle," she dripped all the time, and her husband "was not keen" on it.

Enid had never seriously considered breastfeeding. A short, extremely heavy young woman, she talked to me in her one-bedroom apartment in the project. Her small living room was furnished with a sofa, a single chair, and some shelves. Well-worn, well-scrubbed linoleum covered the floor, and there were many family photos on the walls and shelves as well as drawings Enid's man had done, mostly of her. Throughout our conversation, she sat in the armchair holding her five-month-old son on her lap, a plump, placid baby who never whimpered.

Enid had two miscarriages. When she became pregnant for the third time, she quit her job and stayed home for nine months to make sure nothing would go wrong. The birth itself was not easy. She wanted to have natural childbirth. "I read books about it," she said. "The baby's father went through some of it with me, and he was going to be there for the birth. But I was in labor for two days. The first day the contractions were minor. Then, when I got to the hospital I just chickened out at the last minute. I wanted my mother with me. I didn't want Matt to see me going through so much pain." Her mother did come with her into the delivery room. "She held the baby even before I did," Enid said with a sense of pride.

When I asked what influenced her decision on how to feed the baby, she said, "My own self. I read a bunch of books. The baby's father wanted me to breastfeed, but I didn't go for it."

The week before I talked to her, Enid had returned to her old job as a part-time home health aide. For four hours a day, she visited people who were old or ill in the project, to cook for them and take care of their physical needs. "I went back to work because we needed the money and because I've always worked, since I was in my teens, and I wanted to go back. I was with the baby 24 hours a day before—I took him everywhere with me. I feel very good about him being that close to me."

Her mother, who lives next door, looks after the baby for Enid while she works. He cries for a few minutes when she comes home, almost as if he's angry at her. "I like it when he cries for me," she said. "I want him to know I'm the closest person to him in this world, but I want him to know I can't always be there, too.

"If I had a chance to have some of the things you have, I wouldn't want them," she continued. "I wouldn't want to be white. I like the way I grew up. It taught me that if you want something, you have to work for it. I want to work for what I get; I don't want it to be handed to me. I owe everything to my mother. She's very strong—I remind myself of her a lot."

Matt was doing his share, she acknowledged, taking care of the baby. "This is his baby as much as mine. We do half and half," she said. She planned to get pregnant again "next year" but said that after that she would probably have her tubes tied. Enid said she hoped the next baby would be a girl. Then she smiled as she repeated a popular belief that if the man works harder during intercourse the baby will be a girl, and if the woman works harder it will be a boy. Soon after she pressed me to send her information on a method I had suggested which could increase her chance that the next conception would produce a female child. When I rudely forgot to send it along, she called twice to remind me.

Enid also got her baby's formula from WIC. She doted on the child and when she was home changed his diapers at least once every two hours. As with most of the other women to whom I talked that day, she used disposable diapers. They were expensive, she said, $10 for a box that was used up in about a week and a half. She had no washing machine in the apartment, so for her the convenience and the time saved were well worth it.

"Losing two babies (miscarriages) made me feel empty inside as a woman," she confided to me, "and now I feel complete. I was so blessed when I had this baby. Sometimes peo-

ple say to me that I love him too much. But how could you
love a baby too much?"

For Enid, no trouble is too great to go through for her son—
yet she never considered breastfeeding. Why? At first, since
she was so polite, she found it hard to explain to such a pro-
breastfeeding advocate as myself that the very idea repelled
her. Moreover, she said she was not convinced that breastmilk was better than formula.

Two other women at the community center gave me information about their feeding routines that spanned 20 years and
covered practices in the northern and southern parts of the U.S.
Margaret was attractive, fortyish, dressed in trim lilac pants
and a lilac plaid over-blouse. Barbara was younger, a tall,
straight forward rather heavy-set woman with short hair. Both
had young children at home yet they had very different experiences. Barbara had bottle-fed her first child, but with the next
baby, now a 2-year-old, she tried to breastfeed but failed.

"My girlfriend was breastfeeding as were a couple of other
women I knew," she said, "and they were enthusiastic, so I
wanted to try it. They said it saves the cost of milk. Before the
birth I read up on it, booklets I got from the doctor and from
my girlfriend. I wanted to do it but I wasn't upset that it didn't
work. My baby just wouldn't take the breast; she wouldn't take
the special nursing nipples on bottles either. When she did take
the breast milk, she spit it up." All too soon Barbara gave up
and switched to formula which she got through the WIC program.

As these experiences suggest, when breastfeeding fails we
can't just blame the mother; there are multiple causes. In our
affluent culture we keep babies alive whether or not they can
tolerate their mother's milk. Sanitary and nutritious substitutes abound. But in other, less privileged groups it is not easy.

Speaking of breastfeeding in an evolutionary context, Margaret Mead advised me years ago to watch out for in-
fant/mother pairs who were incompatible with each other,
whose personalities clashed so that they agitated one another,
with the result that the milk supply was affected. "Throughout human history, such babies have died," she commented.

"Shortly, the woman would become pregnant and produce another child who might be more compatible with the mother and survive."

It's possible that if Barbara had persisted, her baby might have accepted the breast. But as it turned out, luckily she had other choices—condensed milk or formula. Had she lived in an Indian or Egyptian village, she might not have had access to a buffalo who had milk to tide her over until she and the baby became adjusted to each other. Her baby would die.

Margaret, my other informant, had considerable experience with both breast- and bottle-feeding. The mother of nine children (the youngest was then five), she explained that she had breastfed the first five and bottle-fed the last four.

Margaret had her five oldest children while she was living in the South, and they were all born at home. "I breastfed the first until he was a year old," she recalled. "I breastfed each of the next four until I got another one. When I found out I might be pregnant, I took them off the breast because I didn't want to give them bad milk. They were born about a year apart." By the time her babies stopped nursing, they were already eating table foods. Margaret generally started them on oatmeal or grits, and then added fruits and home-canned vegetables that she mashed fine. She didn't buy baby foods at that time; it was too expensive for her family.

The last four children were born after Margaret moved north. She had all of them in a hospital. "It was better there," she said, "because you could get needles for the pain. There were no anesthetics at home."

She decided not to breastfeed these babies. "I wanted to try something new, to try bottles. I wanted to see was it different, were the kids fatter or skinnier? But it's the same. The only difference is that you have to buy one and not the other. Breastfeeding is a wonderful feeling, but if I had another child I would use the bottle again." She mentioned that everyone breastfed in the South, that a woman could breastfeed in a public place and no one would stare. In the North, "most of my friends bottle-fed."

We must not slough off these mothers as obedient followers. They were simply adjusting to the lifestyle and social setting in which they lived. Remember that it was not only infant feeding that was different in the urban North or the rural South, it was a whole culture. And when these women found themselves in a new setting, as do we all, they followed patterns that best fit their work and their children's safety. Take for example, the way they arranged the care of their children when they were away. Margaret's husband kept an eye on her youngsters, while a neighbor often baby-sat for Barbara's two. Still they both insisted that for their peace of mind they could not imagine working if it were not for the telephone. Both used the same strategy. The children had to remain in the house and from time to time during the day their mothers would phone home to check on them. "They'd better be there!" Barbara said, and we all laughed knowingly.

Their anecdote reminded me of an incident that occurred some years ago during a trip I made to a project outside New Delhi. A physician, another anthropologist, and I were puzzling over what to do with a supply of surplus food that had been offered to the community to feed the most malnourished children but was refused. The women all agreed that if there wasn't enough for all the children, then none would have it. We talked about letting the mothers decide what was to be done with the food and when we got to the settlement, we told them so. Five women went into a house to discuss it. Within fifteen minutes they returned with the answer. The food would go to the children of the mothers who commuted to work in New Delhi. Not only were these youngsters the most malnourished, but they tended to wander about and get into trouble. Like the intermittent phone calls, they decided to hand out the donated food at different times in the day so that the hungry children would stay close to home, never knowing when it would be their time to eat.

The HLC fieldworker in Houston worked with Mexican-American women (Chicanos) who breastfed their babies while they were living in Mexico but bottle-fed those born in Houston. She tried to support any mother who indicated the slightest interest in breastfeeding. Though some bottle-feeding mothers admitted they would have enjoyed it, they explained

why it was too difficult. On and off, most of them worked outside the home while an older relative or friend cared for their
children. In the summers, they headed north to pick lettuce,
usually leaving the baby behind. A woman named Carmelita
proudly explained to me, "When I went to work upstate with
my husband, we made enough money to pay off the furniture
(she pointed to a couch and two chairs), our TV, *and* the refrigerator." It is imperative that those who work with these
mothers assure them that their choice will not harm their
children; making parents feel guilty for not choosing what *we*
might prefer, puts stress on the mother and ultimately harms
the child.

Carol Bryant, the HLC anthropologist who explored feeding
practices in the Puerto Rican and Cuban community in Dade
County, Florida, reported a similar pattern: women who had
breastfed babies in Puerto Rico and in Cuba felt that to do so
in the United States was out of the question. Some of them
complained that in America they did not have the family support they had at home. Some mentioned the old custom of *la
cuarentena*—a period of postpartum seclusion. In Puerto Rico
and Cuba, when a village woman goes into labor she retires
to a darkened room and remains there. She is coddled and
fussed over for five or six weeks. In the United States, most of
these same women barely had two days to rest before leaving
the hospital and resuming their normal responsibilities.

Of the 81 women who were part of the Florida study, only
a handful were breastfeeding. Most of these mothers switched
to formula or cow milk before the baby's third month, despite
the fact that the majority of them agreed that breastmilk was
best for a baby.

This kind of contradiction is common throughout the world.
The various reasons (rationalizations) women give for choosing the bottle range from "medical problems," such as a Caesarean section or high blood pressure, to insufficient milk. Some
of the Cuban women say that because they lead a hectic, demanding life in the United States, they have a lot of anxiety
which they believe can turn their milk bad and make the baby
sick or at least nervous.

Carol Bryant, with great insight, suggested that the women

were actually relieved to be able to give medical reasons for *not* breastfeeding. Since they believed breastmilk was best for their baby, when they could justify their actions in medical terms it helped them feel a little less guilty.

My small study in Connecticut also included a woman living in a neighborhood in transition, where poor and middle-class families lived side by side. Isabel, one woman I interviewed there, earned over $20,000 a year as an executive secretary. She was Brazilian, married to an American black who was a minister, and they were definitely a couple whose fortunes were rising. Isabel wore her long, dark hair in a French twist and was dressed in tailored slacks and a smart shirt. She had two daughters, Maria, 11, and Rose, 8 months old.

Isabel's first child was born in Brazil when she was in her late teens and unmarried. She didn't breastfeed, partly because she had to take a full-time job just two months after the baby was born. She was the oldest of a large family and supported her mother and younger brothers and sisters by working as an executive secretary at a yacht club. "My mother raised Maria," she explained. "She was closer to her than I was."

A few years ago on a trip to the United States, Isabel met her husband. When they decided to get married, she and her daughter emigrated. He was a man who had never had a family life as a child, and after she got pregnant he became totally absorbed in the pregnancy. "He read more books about pregnancy and infant feeding than I did," Isabel recalled. He wanted her to have natural childbirth, and when it turned out that a Caesarean was necessary, he still insisted on seeing the baby born.

Isabel only breastfed because her husband encouraged her to do it. "I was afraid of the pain," she said, "and that I would lose my shape." However, she found it a very satisfying experience and continued for six months while working part-time. Once the baby was three months old, she used formula to supplement her own milk, but she switched to cow milk at four months because she had raised her older daughter on cow milk and said she had no problems with it.

"In the beginning I was breastfeeding every three hours,"

she recalled. "So every three hours my breasts would start leaking. If I was at the office, it was very embarrassing. I'd say, 'I'm sorry, it's time to go home.' My boss was very understanding." When the baby was six months old, Isabel gave up breastfeeding and returned to full-time work.

She said she's pleased that she breastfed and feels very close to Rose. "I wanted to have this baby as close as possible," she said, intimating how different the situation was when her older daughter was an infant. "I wanted to give her as much of myself as possible."

When Maria is not in school, she can't stop playing with her adored baby sister, and whenever Isabel's husband doesn't have to work he looks after the baby. At other times, they use a baby sitter. His preoccupation with the child has been a mixed blessing. While Isabel was breastfeeding, he worried about her diet and whether she was drinking enough fluids. He'd call her at the office to ask if she had enough to drink and would go to the clinic with her and ask the doctor "all kinds of questions." All this made her feel very much cared for, but there were drawbacks as well.

"In the beginning, he was very possessive about the baby," Isabel explained. "He was making all the decisions. I waited for the right opportunity, then pointed out that I'd had a baby before and he hadn't. Because he knew my mother raised my first child he thought I didn't know any more than he did, but it wasn't so."

Commonly, mothers whose partners are actively involved in child care feel uneasy about it. Each wants to be sure that she comes first with her baby. On the other hand, many are torn because they need help. Such exclusivity is not possible in much of the world, where women are dependent on each other. When a mother can hire a helper, she often feels more in control and thus at ease. The admission of a friend of mine regarding her apprehension is an interesting example of how complex these emotions can be: "I don't mind if Shauna is held by older women," she said of her newborn, "but when women my own age pick her up and take her into another room, I get very upset."

It would be a mistake for any of us to generalize about how mothers feed, especially in as diverse a country as the United States. Many different approaches to infant feeding exist here as in the rest of the world. But if we keep in mind the pervading influence of economic factors on any human endeavor and the value of support in the individual situation, we can spot similar patterns within the same social group. For instance, let me mention three groups with totally different economic and social resources and unique feeding patterns. (Adapted from Raphael 1973).

Upper-middle class and college-educated women today are extremely enthusiastic about breastfeeding because they say it's the "natural" way to feed a baby, but also because many feel a desperate desire for a close, deep relationship in a world they feel is so very impersonal. Even though some of them return to work soon after the birth, still they manage to breastfeed. These days it is not that unusual for a mother to describe how she gets up at dawn to spend half an hour expressing milk with a breast pump so that she can leave those precious ounces behind in a bottle for the baby sitter to feed the baby.

Then there are the women like Roberta who are not college-educated but who are upwardly mobile and share many of the same values as the first group. They agree that breastmilk is best for the baby, and they try to work and still breastfeed, but they don't have as many resources as the more affluent women.

Lastly, we have the women in poverty who are starting from a very different place. To them the bottle is a great convenience and leaves them free when they need to be so they can keep body and soul together in what seems to be an unresponsive world. As I've said earlier, mothers will maximize their baby's health, but if the infant is well and strong and it makes little difference whether he or she gets breastmilk or formula, the mother will most likely make whatever choice favors her own needs.

Today people speak with tolerance or even enthusiasm of breastfeeding. Yet when a woman needs help or advice, often the best the hospital and medical profession can offer is a few pamphlets. And, if she must go out to work, she has another problem. Even though she may have a network of many people she can turn to for help to find housing, a job, or medical assistance, when it comes to child care she's virtually alone if she can't rely on her own mother or a close relative.

More than half the women in the nation have jobs today. Some want to work, but most have no choice because they support or help to support a family. Some working mothers find bottle-feeding is easier. Very few jobs provide infant-care centers on the premises or breastfeeding breaks, no less somewhere they can pump and store their breastmilk. Though the actual emptying of the breasts doesn't take long, the bottles must be clean and sterilized and a refrigerator must be available (often at the work place) so that the pumped milk can be safely stored.

Actually, after a month or so, emptying the breasts every few hours is not critical. However, many Americans still believe it is, based on two erroneous assumptions about breastfeeding: First, if a mother doesn't empty her breasts at regular intervals, her milk supply will fail. And second, given a chance to try both breast and bottle, the baby is bound to prefer a bottle. What these women need to hear is that it is possible to combine the two methods and to maintain their milk supply.

As you have already read, the HLC study found that mothers in other cultures do combine breastfeeding with work. They've had to. Their lot is to supply much of the family food. After a period of time, when the milk is firmly established, the baby is fed other foods during the day and breastmilk at frequent intervals in the early morning and during the night. Mothers often complain their infants refuse non-breastmilk food. But a bottle is a bottle, whether it contains mother's milk or goat milk. The difference is that some parents are more comfortable when the content is homemade.

The WIC program supplied formula for almost all of the mothers I talked with in Waterbridge. WIC was established in most major U.S. cities during the 1970s to provide nutrition information and supplementary foods for pregnant and lactating women and for children up to five years of age. With WIC vouchers a family can buy milk, cheese, eggs, iron-fortified cereals, and other highly nutritious foods, as well as infant formula. The theory behind the program is that individuals who are undernourished in early life are more likely to develop health problems later. Several studies have demonstrated that dollars invested in WIC save tax money that would be spent for Medicaid and other health programs.

Yet the U.S. government remains ambivalent about WIC. As long as American farmers produce a surplus of wheat and other foods, WIC gets support from Congress. However, when products become scarce, legislation to reduce the program is introduced.

More recently, government policy required a percentage of the mothers who are helped at every WIC center to be breast-feeders if that center was to receive its funds. The dictum came down that the woman who breastfeeds not be given formula, which means that for WIC mothers, breastfeeding would become an all-or-nothing proposition. Unfortunately, if women are prevented from supplementing their breastmilk unless they pay for the formula, many are likely to give up breastfeeding even sooner than they had expected.

The argument has been made by government officials that if there were no WIC program to supply mothers with formula, more poor women would be forced to breastfeed. Maybe so. But, as the research attests, some would succeed at it, others would fail and their babies would suffer—as they do in the poor areas of less-developed countries.

We can encourage breastfeeding in the U.S. private sector by indirect methods. For example, we can motivate employers through tax advantages to make it easier for young mothers to nurse their babies. And we can explain to mothers that with the aid of the pediatric community mixed feeding may be preferable to an all-bottle regimen. However, any unilateral attempt to force breastfeeding upon lower income women would be a tragic mistake. You can't legislate breastfeeding.

Eventually the enthusiasm for breastfeeding might spread to currently reluctant American mothers. However, enthusiasm may not be nearly enough. Until more women have the leisure to breastfeed, that is, have a "basic bundle" of adequate housing, food, heat, clothing, and the support they need, few of the patterns described will change.

Certainly, those women who want to breastfeed should be given as much help, encouragement, and knowledge as possible so they may have this warm and most tender of human responses to a child's needs.

7

THE POLITICS OF
BREASTFEEDING

When the HLC study was conceived in 1975 there were just a few researchers concerned with infant feeding in the developing countries. The research has since multiplied a thousandfold. What happened? At the time we were accumulating anthropological evidence from the eleven cultures in which we had studied mothers intimately and in daily life settings, health professionals seeking causes for increased malnutrition and infant mortality started to include breastfeeding within their considerations. More at ease with aggregate statistics and clinical evidence, they assumed, based on conventional hospital data and practical experience, that breastfeeding was on the decline worldwide. Suddenly investigators turned their attention to breastfeeding as if it were an endangered species.

The first surveys which were done in the clinical setting were very naive. Typically they included questions to mothers in a multiple choice format, asking whether they breastfed or bottle-fed. What seemed a sensible approach at the time turned out to be a serious error. We now know mothers usually do both, but we forced them with this kind of research instrument to make a single choice. When researchers did brief, face-to-face interviews with mothers, they were really strangers asking women to *recall* how they had fed their babies, sometimes a year or more earlier. Inevitably, retrospective responses, as they are called, had the mother second-guessing the interviewer's motives and responding with what she thought the interviewer wanted to hear, or what seemed most likely to produce some meager benefit (perhaps some food) for herself and her family.

In search of reasons for this alleged decline, a few investigators suggested there might be a correlation between the tons of baby formula sold and the infant mortality rate—surely the grossest kind of statistical oversimplification. Nonetheless, suspicion was growing among researchers that there was a causal link between infant formula, infant deaths and the reduction or absence of breastfeeding (Jelliffe 1971), a relationship which is still being tested.

This idea of formula as cause entered mainstream thinking in the mid–1970s, a time of great discontent by the more socially-minded with the role and influence of multinational corporations. Their aggressive marketing tactics were seen as linked hand-in-hand with oppressive political regimes and irrational economic development, whose legacy was urbanization and westernization of the worst kind.

A product and its multinational makers, the larger public was told, were now connected with infant deaths and the decline of "natural" or "healthy" feeding practices (Raphael 1976a). So with an anti-formula campaign as an obvious solution, the new politics of breastfeeding emerged—to the astonishment of the company officials who had manufactured and marketed cow milk formula and gained acceptance, nay, the highest of praises from a generation of mothers.

The general public, caught without much knowledge on the plight of Third World women and babies, picked up ideas erratically, often with a popular advocacy slant. Community groups everywhere found themselves being asked to defend mothers and babies with little thought given to the complexity of the issues which surround food policies.

This advocacy position attracted adherents at many levels and from many places. Western and western-trained health professionals, pediatricians, nutritionists, all felt concern. Politicians saw the breastfeeding issue as a way to increase their position either with the companies or by presenting themselves as anti-colonial, anti-industry advocates; academics (ourselves included) responded as much out of curiosity for this new dimension in health research as for the immense possibilities of new funds to revive sagging research programs. United Nations staff concerned with health on a global scale, saw their responsibility immediately. Church-based advocates guessed correctly that the subject of breastfeeding was an opportunity to reach the highest levels and the greatest number of people from the industrial world they were trying to reform.

Finally, in 1981 over 100 member nations of the World Health Organization (WHO), whose delegates are mostly male, signed a resolution which recommended that member nations ban all advertising and promotion of infant formula and other milk products when they are marketed for infant feeding. Only the United States voted no.

The Reagan administration's objection to the WHO resolution had nothing to do with nutrition. The United States argued it was inappropriate for a world assembly to attempt to regulate commercial activity in another country. This stand was later condemned by the U.S. House of Representatives.

Besides "legitimizing" breastfeeding as the ideal feeding for infants in the Third World, the resolution gave credence to a new set of rationalizations which condoned: a specific number of months as the appropriate time for the introduction of supplementary food; the value of exclusive breastfeeding; and the belief in "no cost" value of breastfeeding. Indirectly, they implied there was a right way and a wrong way to feed and that we would do well to be wary of the feeding decisions of poor ignorant mothers.

These interesting premises were the basis for constraints adopted by advocacy groups in the United States, England and elsewhere, which would have the effect of reducing women's options in their method of feeding. Attempts were made to eliminate bottles in hospitals; cut back on exports designed for infants; change infant formula advertising; restrict a mother's access to bottles or any breastmilk substitutes in the marketplace; link aid programs for welfare mothers to breastfeeding practices; and, back programs which would attempt to convince mothers that for the sake of their babies they should breastfeed.

A bill was introduced into the U.S. House of Representatives constraining the sale of infant formula by American companies overseas. More likely than not, none of these constraints would have had much effect on the infant feeding patterns of women in poor countries since they did not include the local and national companies who, for the most part, vastly outsell the imported milk companies. For example, the gigantic Amul Milk Company in Rajastan, India, a cooperative "owned" by 300,000 families, sells most of the processed milk in that part of the country. Foreign imported products account for only a very small percentage of India's commercial milk market.

Some delegates to the World Health Organization sensibly urged incentives for mothers, such as breastfeeding breaks, paid maternity leave, flexible work schedules and day-care centers. However, a few advocated medical prescriptions for formula and feeding bottles. New Guinea now has a law which bans the sale of feeding bottles and nipples without a prescription.

After nearly a decade of accusations, meetings, compromises and ill-will, and millions of words in the media, Nestlé, the largest infant formula producer in the world and the primary target of this campaign in the United States, though they do not market formula here, agreed to honor the WHO code of advertising practices. They convinced Senator Edmund Muskie, a man of unchallenged integrity, to chair a commission which would monitor Nestlé activity worldwide. This diffused the issue and within a year or so, Nestlé officials and their critics were shaking hands. One major episode in this highly emotional and most complex world issue was removed from the larger scene, but its impact on policy institutions and the direction of research on food has yet to be measured.

In hindsight, we can say there is much to regret in what the so-called breast/bottle controversy did not do for mothers and the strain it put on the civility among professionals. Physicians forgot about mothers as they argued in an either/or context about the values of breast and bottle at conferences and in their journals; politicians held congressional hearings and purposefully looked for scapegoats whom they charged with foul play. Health professionals became advocates instead of resource people or counselors taking positions rather than listening to patients with the emphasis centered mainly on infants, leaving out the mothers. Likewise, the distribution of food to the hungry, seldom formula and mostly dried milk, was jeopardized. The product was to suffer for the sins of the producer.

This decade of revelations released centuries of shyness, inhibition and ignorance about lactation. It was as if a new human function had come upon the world, exciting the imagination and demanding information. It was part of our responsibility at the Lactation Center, as a public agency, to respond to this thirst for understanding about breastfeeding. And so we did. We answered thousands of queries stimulated by the controversy. In the process, we realized it would be important to study the effects of this interesting conflict in relation to our own research. So over the years the use and misuse by the media of the data which our team of anthropologists had so carefully collected was analyzed. Overall, angry critics used the insights we published to develop opposing theories that would support their point of view; industry used our findings on mothers in poverty to justify their position which denied that they were responsible for all the dying babies.

It took us years to convince all parties concerned that we at the Center held a third point of view—neither pro- nor anti-industry, pro- nor anti-advocacy. Our position was to speak for the women who were subject and object of this international investigation and to explain the so-called "decline" of breastfeeding *in their terms. That's what this book is all about.*

8

MATERNAL WISDOM

It may be surprising but the ten-year battle between the companies that market infant formula and their critics had some very positive and useful results. The controversy alerted professionals and the general public as well about the virtues of breastfeeding. As a result, today women who want to breastfeed are not only "permitted" this choice but encouraged to do so. Much of the subsequent research on the effects of breastmilk on the human infant gut was stimulated by the conflict, findings not only significant in their own right but valuable as a justification for promoting breastfeeding.

Information on lactation, the biological as well as the social aspects, has come into the public domain and become a part of our folklore. (Perhaps for the first time in human history, men have been privy to such extensive intimacies about matters of reproduction and breastfeeding.) We have come a long way. A few years ago, when I wrote *The Tender Gift: Breastfeeding* (1976b), it offered mothers who would breastfeed permission to do so. Certainly the commotion engendered by this international debate reaffirmed that gift.

A whole new cluster of eye-opening insights surfaced which lent itself to practical actions. There emerged a deep appreciation of the complexity of this subject and a keen awareness of the essential part economic, social and demographic factors play in determining feeding practices. A new holistic view of breastfeeding came into being.

One highlight was a better understanding of the nature of the support women require in order to breastfeed successfully and raise their children safely. Still another came from the analysis of our team reports about the practices of mixed feeding and weaning. All of these discoveries contributed partial answers to our questions about the perceived decline in breastfeeding and what appeared to be a contradiction—an improvement in infant health.

A good example of the complex nature of this issue comes from the HLC staff's attempt to answer some straightforward questions: How much commercial milk was distributed, when was it delivered, to which overseas countries, and where was it sold? Much to our surprise we found that the companies that processed and sold the milk had records of the number of units that left their factories but, after that, the intermediate processes—the trucking to the docks, the loading of the cases onto hundreds of different ships, the stops at dozens of different ports, the unloading of unequal units at each stop, the deliveries to the various distribution agents from the dock (each of different amounts), and the sale of the milk through a series of middlemen to the shopkeepers—made any final figures no more than educated guesses based on the available data. In other words, your guess is as good as mine.

We turned to the United Nations for infant mortality statistics and found ourselves in a similar dilemma. Who knew then that the world census figures were based on reports from only 42 percent of the member countries and that the figures were approximate at best. Curiosities were exposed. One country's mortality figures were exactly the same two years in a row! And we heard tell of the sister of a head of state, who, shocked by her country's high infant mortality figures, had reduced them by half.

Contrary to popular beliefs, the figures revealed a decline in infant and maternal mortality in the last two decades but, surprisingly, an increase in adult male mortality. The folk wisdom so often reported in our field data supported the demographic trend on child survival. Again and again, older women sang the virtues of the good old days, but, when pressed further, sadly admitted that far more of their children died than their daughters' children.

Since the presence of a baby takes so much of a woman's time and energy, she quite naturally needs added help for herself because, surprising as it may seem, breastmilk comes at a cost. Gone are the days when we could assume that milk flows no matter what the mother's circumstances, that child care is relatively energy free, and that a woman's time is of no value unless she is actually working for wages outside the home. In fact, a poor woman's major asset may be her time. The hours she invests in breastfeeding inevitably mean less time available to weed the garden that feeds her family or to search out odd jobs that will pay for food and housing.

William Butz, now with the U. S. Bureau of Census, calculated the "true" cost of breastfeeding (1977). He balanced the money a woman saves by breastfeeding (that she might otherwise spend on food for the baby) against the money she needs to earn if she is to supply the extra nutrients she requires to have enough breastmilk for the baby and food for her other children. He concluded that for many of the world's urban poor the economic cost of breastfeeding far outweighs the benefits. We are not repeating the results of this study to suggest that women in poor urban areas should not breastfeed. They should; in fact they must. But, we must also understand the trade-off that has to be made, so that if we are ever put in a position to make decisions about the lives of these women, we are able to do so intelligently.

Clearly, malnutrition in infants is linked to income, not to the choice women made between bottle-feeding and breast-feeding. In one rural area of Jamaica, a researcher found the extent of malnutrition in a family was directly related to the amount of money the family had available for food (Marchione 1980). Obviously, poverty is not good for children.

Repeatedly, we were faced with the puzzle of why some mothers, even in the same socioeconomic environment, are more likely to be successful at breastfeeding than others. The intimate profiles we discuss in these pages reveal that women in traditional cultures need support just as much as mothers in suburban America and that it is available to some women some of the time but not to every woman all the time. As we have shown over and again, mothers need to be mothered if they are to succeed in breastfeeding.

The HLC data gave explicit evidence that in traditional cultures, where breastfeeding is still universal, there are strict prescriptions regarding the support of new mothers from one or more close relatives—the person we have referred to as the *doula*. Several recent studies have analyzed the function of the doula who supports the breastfeeding mother: midwife or other health professional who plays that role (Raphael 1981); older women in traditional cultures (WHO 1981); and paid workers in a low income urban area in Kentucky (Bryant 1981). A unique "doula project" in Guatemala showed that women who have a doula with them in the delivery room tend to breastfeed for more months than those who do not (Sosa 1980).

A comparison of new American mothers who were encouraged to breastfeed while in the hospital with women who were not prodded to do so revealed that they did breastfeed as long as they were in the hospital, but they did not necessarily continue to breastfeed once they returned to their home. The research revealed that three months later they were no more likely to be breastfeeding than the mothers who had not been approached (Newton 1984). Similar patterns, where elaborate supportive help fostered breastfeeding but where breastfeeding stopped once the support ended, were reported for Chile (Raphael and King 1977) and the Philippines (Popkin in press).

Usually, with the appropriate support, the women in the various cultures we studied could breastfeed for many months provided they had enough to eat and were under no pressure to breastfeed exclusively. In addition, we observed that the successful breastfeeders were not obsessed with conforming to a predetermined hourly feeding scheme for so many weeks or months.

These findings made us realize that new mothers and those who would support and counsel them would have to reevaluate some of the old premises and invent new prescriptions for feeding, especially in the urban areas. The challenge is to find regimens that fit breastfeeding comfortably into daily lives rather than prescribe programs that jam life schedules into a rigid pattern of feeding. In fact, since success at breastfeeding can often be predicted based on the presence of (or lack of) a supportive network (Raphael 1976b), we at least have a model to build on. But that judgment needs to include a thorough

18. A patriarch from the Moslem community in Trinidad poses with his grandchildren. "When I can't get this government to deliver water to the village, I feel shame," he admitted.

19. A man's commitment to his children is as strong in traditional societies as anywhere else; an example of care-giving in Cairo.

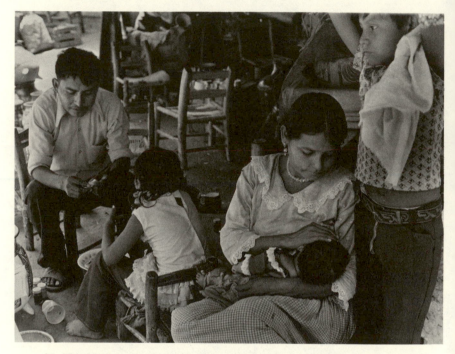

20. This Mexican family personifies a major theme of Margaret Mead's keynote address for the First International Conference on Breastfeeding. Entitled "The Family Context of Breastfeeding," she stressed that the breastfeeding "unit" is a woman, her baby, and the supportive network (usually of family members) around her.

understanding of the sensitive function of breastfeeding and a realistic appreciation of the problems surrounding additional food.

Observing women feed and recording all the nuances of that behavior taught us never to accept simple descriptions of infant feeding patterns, for family interactions, interruptions, the health of the mother, the quantity of food available, the season of the year are all significant, and all make a difference. It's apparent that the conventional view among health professionals (until recently) that most women could breastfeed for at least six months, perhaps even a year, without supplementing their breastmilk was a gross misjudgment. We are still far from understanding what mothers do, no less what we should caution them to do. Authorities are divided between those who believe babies must be given supplements around three months to keep up their strength (Ghosh 1981, Waterlow 1981), and those who insist that mothers should feed the baby only breastmilk until six months, trading off growth for safety against environmental contamination and diarrhea (Habte 1982).

Yet, early on in our study, as the fieldworkers' notes began to come in, we were struck by the evidence that breastfeeding women in traditional cultures gave their babies all kinds of food in very small amounts at an early age, in some cases when the infant was just 2 weeks old. At three or four months in most communities, parents introduced semi-solids made from corn, rice, or whatever was available, a practice we had thought was only for older babies.

Mixed feeding—breastmilk and additional food—appeared to be the common, everyday feeding regimen for the one- to 6-month-old child. This pattern was also reported as the norm five years later in most of the cultures surveyed by a WHO-UNICEF study. We began to appreciate why mothers in these countries worry as much about finding additional foods for their young as they do about their breastmilk supply.

When we first reported these activities few people were ready to accept our descriptions; if women could breastfeed, there seemed to be no logical reason for them to give their babies other foods. But now we know more. The reader can refer to Chapter 2 where we describe how a research team, measuring the supply of breastmilk in women of different cultures, reported that it usually levels off at about three months. To keep the baby growing from then on, mothers automatically supplement their supply.

Obviously most of the world's women do not follow calendars or the mandates of popular advice. They breastfeed and, without fuss, give their infants other foods when they seem to want it; babies want it increasingly by month three. In fact, even before the third month, there are periods when additional foods may be necessary because of the fragility of a woman's health, her emotional life, activity level and even her water intake, not to mention the fluctuations in appetite and the sporadic growth spurts of the child. So it's natural for her to follow an open-ended pattern, moving from nursing to additional foods and back to breastmilk.

No two women are alike and breastmilk can reach a maximum volume early or, as often happens for some women, much later than three months. We observed that if a mother needed to supplement earlier she did so without feelings of failure or guilt. If she could continue exclusively on breastmilk beyond three months, she did.

Breastfeeding as practiced by most mothers, then, is essentially a composite of behaviors. It is a series of actions with breastmilk production a serious concern but with additional foods an equally important pressure. Usually these indigenous foods are composed of cooking water and mashed starchy vegetables from the family pot. Most of these semi-liquid or *beikost* foods, as they are called, are low in protein, high in bulk, and not very palatable. However, even a small amount of human or animal milk added to these local foods changes the chemistry, greatly enhancing the nutritive value of these starchy paps. That is why it is prudent for a mother to continue to breastfeed even if her milk supply is limited. Other milk, animal or processed, remains beyond the reach of most poor women unless it is subsidized by government. Putting it very clearly, although breastfeeding has been the issue all along, weaning food is an equally grave problem.

It would be foolhardy to think that all that is needed to end malnutrition is to manufacture some combination of the traditional foods (grains with vegetables) used by local women. Not so. While it is possible to make highly nutritious preparation from indigenous foods (Cameron & Hofvander 1971), and hundreds have been tried (Orr 1972), they are an innovation, costly in fuel, water, machinery and ingredients. Most attempts have failed.

No inexorable link exists between healthy babies and cultures where breastfeeding is the norm. In fact, of all the communities in the HLC study, the Egyptian and Indian villages with the highest rate of mortality were also the communities where virtually all the mothers breastfed for long periods of time with the least amount of additional weaning foods. The mortality rate was not caused by breastfeeding, but occurred in spite of it. On the other hand, the mothers we studied in Texas and in Florida used bottles more than all the other groups. Their babies had the lowest incidence of illness and hardly any deaths were recorded. No question this was not because the infants were bottle-fed, but because their families had refrigerators, safe water, adequate health care, prenatal medical attention and a decent diet.

A lot of energy has gone into multi-million dollar programs to promote breastfeeding, but we still have hungry babies. As we have argued, the heart of the problem is that many researchers are not in touch with the reality of what breastfeeding mothers do, so their decisions are frequently inappropriate. Only mothers know that "weaning is always" and that mixed feeding is the method. We are counting on future anthropological (and other) research to reveal the subtleties of infant feeding practices.

Since the social, economic and demographic profile of mothers can influence their style of feeding, it should be no surprise to the reader that similar types of infant feeding patterns can be found in totally different cultures (Raphael 1973). In fact, it is helpful to cluster some of the cultures when analyzing the data and trying to uncover patterns of culture change.

For example, we have identified the traditional, usually village, societies where virtually all mothers breastfeed. As our stories have shown with women in Egypt or Rani in India, they breastfeed because they cannot afford to do otherwise and they do it without much difficulty where they have sufficient family support—economic and social.

The style of breastfeeding among the elite in Western societies is another pattern. We need no example of these affluent upper middle class American women for this book. They are all too familiar. What is interesting is that professionals, whether in England, India, Nigeria or New Orleans, exhibit similar patterns. These mothers generally have leisure time to breastfeed and they regard it as a valuable and pleasurable experience. They choose to breastfeed though they have other choices. They feel that breastfeeding makes them better women, better mothers and that it strengthens the bond between themselves and their children. But, even if they should choose not to breastfeed, they can afford processed milk and will have healthy babies.

Not so with the urban poor, our third type of social arrangement. These women live in rapidly changing urban communities. They will breastfeed, but a study of their lives day in and day out reveals that their major concern is survival—to have enough money to buy rice for the day's meal, or shoes so a son can go to school or a salve to cure an infected eye.

These urban poor are caught in an extraordinary bind. They prefer to live in the city for a long list of reasons. They may or may not have better living conditions than they had in the rural communities from which they came, but the health services and schooling for their children are compelling attractions. Unquestionably, life in the city offers a more varied diet, a diverse and stimulating environment, as well as a chance to escape burdensome kinship obligations.

On the other hand, their network of relatives and friends frequently stops short of help with baby care. Some relatives are too far away and too poor to travel; those who are close are often too involved in their own struggle and can't afford the time.

Besides, many of these mothers are the sole support of their family. For them the pressures of their household workloads (plus a job outside the home) leaves them little leisure time to breastfeed. All too often breastfeeding is an early casualty since lactation is a sensitive human function, readily disrupted and quickly abandoned when a woman's lifestyle can no longer accommodate it. Infant feeding practices are part of a broader process of social change that occurs as poor people become urbanized; frequently that stage of development precludes the practice of breastfeeding.

And that was a surprise. Something about breastfeeding doesn't work for these women, whether they are new immigrants to the city in less developed countries (those citified women whom the Indian and Egyptian village wives look down upon and chide as being bad mothers) or immigrants from rural America who move to a northern city (remember Margaret, who breastfed five children in her home community in the South but bottle-fed the next four in Bridgewater). Is it possible that as the developing world takes on Western values, the trend to the bottle may be irresistible, even inevitable, unless we can find a way to protect, sustain and support mothers during this vital period?

Much as we might hope otherwise, these mothers are turning to bottle-feeding in the same way that women of industrialized nations did from the turn of the century on. Attempts to stem the tide away from breastfeeding did not work. The country's most distinguished pediatricians, E. Emmett Holt, Sr., and his son, who were the "Spocks" of the early 1900s, pleaded with women to continue breastfeeding, but they turned to bottles *en masse* (Raphael 1966). Only when a substantial breastfeeding elite developed among better educated, more affluent women in the 1960s did the pattern begin to reverse itself.

Well-intended pleas failed to stop women from doing what they believed was right then, and it is unlikely that campaigns which promote actions that do not fit this generation's needs, regardless of social class, will work any better. Women will ultimately act in their own best interests and decide how to feed their babies according to what their lives allow. Their greatest stumbling blocks are the indifference of other human beings, the lack of concern of our governments and the insidious effects of the major culprit—poverty. Current international food policy remains insensitive to the need for more, not fewer, feeding options.

A few last words.

Breastmilk is best. Few would disagree, yet in many countries we know that infant mortality drops when women improve the quality and quantity of weaning foods, or when, with all the benefits of health and sanitation that western culture has invented, they move from breastfeeding to bottle-feeding. Remember, it is not "the bottle" that magically saves lives but what a family can afford to do that keeps a child healthy.

Twenty years ago, looking at the trend away from breastfeeding by the urban poor and then back to breastfeeding by the elite, Margaret Mead said to me, "Find a way that we can go from the peasant and working class breastfeeder to the elite, well-educated breastfeeder without a generation of bottles in between." I've been trying ever since.

If we were to preach for new directions, this much we can say: Let's rid ourselves of preconceptions about breastfeeding as "natural" and thus easy ("Sometimes the baby wanted to breastfeed all day long and I was so tried"); about traditional, rural cultures as places where breastfeeding is universal and exclusive ("Breastfeeding made me feel too tied down"); where family ties are close and loving ("I didn't want to ask my mother-in-law every time I wanted to leave the house"); and, where people live undisturbed pastoral lives ("I wasn't going to be a shepherd's wife"). Of course, there is happiness but there is also boredom, excruciatingly hard work ("When I came up here, I worked so hard, I had to clean 20 offices but it's better than pickin' cotton") and never enough money ("I asked my sister to give me a shilling for some milk but she didn't have it").

The challenge is to get away from thinking in absolute terms about feeding practices, from assuming that it must be breast or bottle, total breastfeeding or none at all, and to avoid authoritarian ideas about what's best for women and babies in our own or somebody else's culture.

For example from an earlier chapter: Joyce's first child was not breastfed; the second was breastfed for 9 months, she stopped because she was pregnant; the third for 14 months; the fourth, 6 months, and she stopped when the baby went to the hospital for a hernia operation; she stopped nursing the fifth at 14 months because he kept waking her at night; the sixth, well, she wasn't sure, for she was going to take birth control pills. She fed all of them evaporated milk from two weeks on, and soft foods soon after.

It requires that we become more tolerant. Can't we appreciate that some women cannot or will not choose to breast-feed? Breastfeeders were abused years ago when it was out of fashion, so let's be wary of any blatant campaign to convince mothers that they have an obligation to provide breastmilk for their children just because it is in fashion. Most edicts and dictums, and those who promote them, are far too distant from the child-rearing scene to intrude on this highly personal decision. Pressure and guilt are counter-productive and add another stress to the mother/child interaction.

If anything, we must also become more situational in our outlook about feeding behavior, paying attention to such important variables as a mother's lifestyle, her partner's economic status, her network of support, and the amount, availability and accessibility of foods for her and her infant.

We seek a holistic view for the remedies and policies we devise to protect the health and welfare of mothers as well as babies. They are useless if they are not based on the realities of mothers in poverty, women in transition, working women and determined women.

These women have the right to make their own choices about how to feed their infants—just as we do—and most will act wisely, just as we would. To do otherwise wrongly foists our bias onto others and endangers the health of babies.

For the benefit of mothers everywhere, we have argued that over time most feeding episodes are rooted in the economics of the family and that mothering styles are far more important than officially sanctioned or fashionable feeding modes. For the sake of this generation of mothers, we hope these powerful personal life histories will persuade government officials, health ministers and others who make decisions about breastmilk and other food, of the need to develop more flexible and humane food policies.

If we are to help these mothers, we must trust them and acknowledge that they are important beyond their reproductive roles; that they are more than just a food supply for infants. Wherever we have gone, we have found mothers who knew better than we what it takes to keep babies alive. After the agonies of several bitter decades of hunger and malnutrition, we would be foolish to deny the survivors a chance to voice their point of view in any forum—local or international. The evidence suggests that the participation of mothers, sophisticated or peasant, will maximize their well being and the health and survival of their infants.

BIBLIOGRAPHY

Bryant, Carol Anne. "The Impact of Kin, Friend and Neighbor Networks on Infant Feeding Practices." *Soc. Sci. Med.*, 16 (1982),
1765.

Butz, William P. "Economic Aspects of Breastfeeding." Paper delivered at Conference on Nutrition and Reproduction. February
12–16, 1977, Washington, D.C.

Cameron, Margaret, and Yngve Hofvander. *Manual on Feeding Infants and Young Children*. New York: Protein Advisory Group
of the United Nations System, PAG Document 1.14/26 (1971).

Cole, E. "Tonnage—A Poor Measure of Trend to Bottle Feeding." *The
Lactation Review*, 5:1 (1980), 3.

Ely, F., and W. E. Peterson. "Factors Involved in the Ejection of Milk."
Journal of Dairy Science 24 (1941), 211.

Fairley, Nancy J. "Reproductive Decision-Making Among Black
Women: Cultural Issues for Health Practitioners." Paper delivered at the American Anthropological Association, December 1981, Los Angeles, Calif.

Franklin, Robert. Letter describing research by himself, Frank Baer,
and William Bertrand. January 14, 1982.

Frisch, R. E. "Population, Food Intake and Fertility." *Science* 199
(1978), 22–30.

Ghosh, Shanti. "Faltering in Infant Growth in Less Developed Countries." *The Lancet* (January 31, 1981), 281.

Habte, Demissie. Discussion at the International Pediatric Association Conference on Infant Feeding Practice, November 27, 1983,
Ankara, Turkey.

Huffman, Sandra L., A.K.M. Alauddin Chowdhury, J. Chakraborty
and W. Henry Mosley. "Nutrition and Post-Partum Amenor-

rhoea in Rural Bangladesh." *Population Studies* 32: 2 (1977),
251–259.

Jelliffe, D. B. "Commerciogenic Malnutrition? Time for a Dialog." *Nutr.
Rev.* 30 (1972), 199.

Marchione, Thomas J. "A History of Breastfeeding in the English-
Speaking Caribbean in the Twentieth Century." *Food and Nutrition Bulletin* 2: 2 (1980), 9–18.

Newton, Laura. Personal Communication, 1984.

Newton, Niles. Personal Communication, 1965.

Orr, Elizabeth. "The Use of Protein-rich Foods for the Relief of Malnutrition in Developing Countries: An Analysis of Experience." London: Tropical Products Institute G73 (1972).

Popkin, Barry M. *Proceedings, NIFAC Conference on Breastfeeding
and Infant Nutrition.* New York: Praeger Special Studies (In
press).

Puffer, Ruth R. "Breastfeeding in Latin American Projects" In
Breastfeeding and Food Policy in a Hungry World, Dana Raphael, ed., New York: Academic Press (1979).

Puffer, Ruth R., and Carlos V. Serrano. "Results of the Inter-Ameri-
can Investigations of Mortality Relating to Reproduction."
Bulletin of the Pan American Health Organization, 10: 2 (1976).

Raphael, Dana. "The Lactation-Suckling Process in the Matrix of
Supportive Behavior." Ph.D. thesis, Columbia University Mi-
crofilm #69–15,580 (1966).

———. "The Role of Breastfeeding in a Bottle-Oriented World." *Ecology of Food and Nutrition* 2 (1973), 121–126.

———. "Warning: The Milk in This Container May be Lethal for Your
Infant." In *Medical Anthropology*, F. X. Grollig and H. Haley,
eds. The Hague: Mouton; Chicago: Aldine, (1976a), 129–136.

———. *The Tender Gift: Breastfeeding.* New York: Schocken Books,
1976b.

———. "The Midwife as Doula: A Guide to Mothering the Mother."
Journal of Nurse-Midwifery, November/December (1981), 13–
15.

———. Weaning Is Always: The Anthropology of Breastfeeding Behavior." *Ecology of Food and Nutrition* 15 (1984), 203–213.

Raphael, Dana, and Joyce King. "Mothers in Poverty: Breastfeeding
and the Maternal Struggle for Infant Survival." *The Lactation
Review* 2: 3 (1977).

Rowland, M.G.M., Alison A. Paul and R. G. Whitehead. "Lactation
and Infant Nutrition." *British Medical Bulletin* 37: 1 (1981),
77–82.

Sosa, R., et al. "The Effect of a Supportive Companion on Perinatal Problems, Length of Labor, and Mother-Infant Interaction." *New England Journal of Medicine* 303 (1980), 597–600.

Stack, Carol. *All Our Kin.* New York: Harper & Row, 1974.

Waterlow, J. D. "Faltering in Infant Growth in Less Developed Countries." *The Lancet* (January 31, 1981), 281.

Whitehead, R. G., A. A. Paul and M.G.M. Rowland. "Lactation in Cambridge and in The Gambia." In *Topics in Paediatrics* 2, Nutrition in Childhood. B. A. Wharton, ed., Tunbridge Wells: Pitman Medical (1980), 22–32.

WHO. *Contemporary Patterns of Breastfeeding.* Report on WHO Collaborative Study on Breastfeeding. World Health Organization, Geneva, 1981.

WHO/UNICEF. Joint WHO/UNICEF Meeting on Infant and Young Child Feeding, Geneva, October 9–12, 1979 (World Health Organization, Geneva 1979).

INDEX

Abortion, 106
Agriculture, vegetable gardens: in the Philippines, 26-27; in the Sardinian mountain village, 75-76, 79-80
AID Breastfeeding project, xiv, 5, 9; findings of, 137-148
Amul Milk Company, 134
Arapesh, 34

Black women in America, 115-129; infant feeding practices of, 115-128; support networks for, 127; working patterns of, 127
Books, as source of breastfeeding information, 118, 120
Bottle-feeders: contempt of village women towards, 49, 50, 64, 73, 82; guilt in, 117
Bottle-feeding: attitudes towards, 49, 50, 73; danger of, 133; reasons for, 92, 99, 123; trends in, 144-145; by urban poor, 144-145; in the United States, 146. *See also* Weaning

Breast, as sexual object, 35
Breast/bottle-feeding: controversy, 132, 134; U.S. statistics of, 115
Breastfeeding: attitudes of women in traditional society, 21, 34, 72, 77, 83, 90; attitudes of women in U.S., 21, 115, 146; campaign in St. Kitts, 110; complexity of, 138, 146; contraceptive effect of, 37, 65; cultural practices of, 6, 56; decline of, 23, 49, 77, 132; duration of, 23, 37, 49, 50, 64, 66, 67, 77, 99, 141; economics of, 139; ejection reflex in, 83, 88; food for mother during, 36; holistic view of, 147; informational books on, 116; learning about, 97; male encouragement of, 73, 124; male knowledge of, 81, 86, 124; and ovulation, 37, 65; painful nipples during, 34; politics of, 131-135; during pregnancy, 65; by other women, 34, 64, 82; rationalizations for, 83,

About the Authors

DANA RAPHAEL has written the now classic *The Tender Gift: Breastfeeding* and many popular and scholarly articles, and has edited *Being Female: Reproduction, Power, and Change* and *Breastfeeding and Food Policy in a Hungry World*. Dr. Raphael is the director of The Human Lactation Center, Ltd., which she founded with Margaret Mead in 1975.

FLORA DAVIS is an established writer whose works have appeared in numerous mass circulation magazines. She is the author of *Inside Intuition, Eloquent Animals,* and *Living Alive!*

Ar